Study
WAR
No
More

Study War No More

A Peace Handbook for Youth

Edited by David S. Young

Brethren Press: Elgin, Illinois

Acknowledgement is given to United Feature Syndicate, Inc. for permission to reproduce a PEANUTS cartoon.

Art Work by Kathy Kline
Editing by Bob Bowman

Contents

PREFACE

David S. Young

In teenage years, great decisions of life are being made. It has been my dream to have a resource that would help youth make a decision to use their lives for peace. As a pastor, I have been keenly aware that there is no small handbook to help youth understand one of the central beliefs of the Church of the Brethren. Our teachings of peace sometimes are sporadic, too intellectual, or outside of youth circles.

This booklet has been prepared with a youth audience in mind. It can be adapted to camp, youth meeting, or Sunday school setting. Each chapter has questions for discussion or activities that can stimulate the reader to consider the issues. Our hope is that this guide would become a hip-pocket resource for many settings.

I want to acknowledge the many who have made this handbook possible. First, Chuck Boyer and Bob Bowman of the Elgin Offices of the Church of the Brethren and M. R. Zigler of New Windsor, founder of On Earth Peace, who urged me to make such a dream become reality. Then I thank each person who so willingly agreed to write a chapter. Special thanks to Kathy Kline of Brethren Volunteer Service for her illustrations.

Finally, and certainly not least, I thank my grand-mother, Lydia Price Wolf; my mother, Grace Wolf Young; and my uncle, Pastor Bruce Anderson for teaching me peace in the home; Pastor Glen Norris and Pastor Glenn Kinsel for teaching me peace in the church; Camp Swatara and Southern District of Pennsylvania youth for district experiences. And finally to my wife Joan Reznar Young who, on coming into the Church of the Brethren, continually asked why we don't emphasize more the teachings on peace of the Church of the Brethren.

To the end that peace begins in our hearts as we respond to Christ, this handbook is shared. It is dedicated to all who would be makers of peace and the above-mentioned peacemakers in my life.

Decision for Peace
David S. Young

I was a freshman at Elizabethtown College, majoring in math with a full schedule. It was a full sixteen hours of classes a week, with chemistry lab and Chapel Choir squeezed in. I had enrolled in college after high school and was living in the men's dormitory on that lovely Pennsylvania colonial campus.

Those were not the easiest months. To the upper classmen we were known as "Frosh," short for freshman, and in that day we were forced to wear little hats known as dinks. We removed them courteously when upper classmen passed, and many made fun of our disadvantaged status. With the usual homesickness, grades to pull, and new friendships to establish, most freshmen had enough to face. I was like any other youth just out of high school, facing life now on my own.

Then came the event that was to highlight the anxiety of this season. I received a call from the office of the Dean of Men, Ed Crill, at that time. The occasion was my 18th birthday, and I was soon to find out the significance of that birthday during the days of the draft. A young man had to register his intention regarding the military. If I wanted to register as a Conscientious Objector, one who opposes participation in war, it was very important to register that intention on the initial form. It was fortunate that I received the call that day. In all the newness of the situation I may have missed what the law required on my 18th birthday, registration for the draft.

Without any particular preparation, in fact with only my childhood training, I entered the dean's office. Because I was going to a Church of the Brethren college, the office personnel were familiar with my background. The Church of the Brethren, one of the historic peace churches, was founded over 250 years ago. It teaches its youth and adults that God wants peace for the world. From childhood I had been taught that Christ taught an alternative to the use of violence. As Christians we would use peaceful means to settle differences in every situation in life.

I worked at filling in my form. The office personnel assisted me in several questions, because I had never seen such a form. I found my training had been thorough, but I just never thought of actually facing the day to declare my intentions. It's like getting your driver's license at 16. As much as you look forward to that day, when you finally get in the car for the exam with a state trooper at your side, you get a little edgy. It's all very real at that moment. In the case of registration, I signed the dotted line with my decision to be a conscientious objector.

A MANUAL OF INSTRUCTION

Just as in preparing for a driver's test there is a manual of instruction, so this book can be a manual of instruction for the peace position of the New Testament as taught by Jesus. My hope would be that it would be a resource for helping youth understand the position of the Christian who chooses an alternative to war, to tell how that intention is registered, and how peace can be lived out. We will survey the teachings of the Master and look for his way of handling differences, large and small.

Jesus taught and also lived the way of peace.

This book tells the story of how people have translated these teachings into action in face of war and in building for peace. It witnesses to how youth have decided to live by their ideals, taking up very concrete projects for peace. It tells how those projects influenced them throughout life. Pacifism does not remove us from ordinary events of life. It is a way of constructively dealing with the conflicts that emerge.

We soon learn that the ideal of peace affects every aspect of living. In fact, I believe it has been in daily events that I learned the lesson. The teaching of peace influences our homes, the climate in our church, and the way we treat friend and foe alike. Peacemaking is not as much a decision about military service at time of war as it is building a positive lifestyle for handling conflict. The Gospel record becomes so much more complete as we see the Prince of Peace at work through our lives.

DO YOU BELIEVE IN DRIVING?

The scope of this book goes beyond the manual of instruction for driving. Most persons believe in driving. It is not a decision of conscience to get into that car and drive. Making the decision of how to register for the draft, on the other hand, involves us in clarifying our basic values. The decision forces us to ask, "What do I really believe about life and its purpose? What will my life stand for?" The decision shapes a course of behavior. How do I approach disagreements? Do I try to work at peaceful methods of solving conflict? Do I believe in killing? What is the meaning of human life, my life? Whether the draft is in effect or not, each person must decide his or her life's direction.

SHAPE UP OR BE SHAPED

Longfellow once wrote that in this world one must either be an anvil or a hammer. Either we are molded and swayed by all that goes on around, or we can become a part of a vision that shapes the world. This book hopes to challenge the best of our thoughts and energies with the age old call of Jesus to be peacemakers. How can we stand for peace in a world with neutron bomb, a bomb which can kill people and leave foliage unharmed? Who will have the courage to beat swords into plowshares and military budgets into food for the hungry of the world? How can scientific advancement be made to be the servant of a new age of international harmony where nation will not lift up sword against nation? What is the call of conscience in regard to solutions of world problems? And very personally, what is the call in terms of the use of my own intellect and talents in regard to the one life I have to live?

Finally, the way of peace will not be popular nor easy to apply. In fact, pressure from others about your peace stand may make you feel on the outside. Like being a college freshman, this ideal may cause others to snicker or to ridicule. At that point such treatment may feel very harsh. A resource like this can bolster our courage by helping us to clearly define our stand and also to see that many others made their witness in the face of odds. We can feel a unity with a tradition and learn from its experience.

LIVE A VISION

We can feel challenged to build a church where peace is not only taught but also lived. Our homelife and our communities can be changed as we apply the Christian alternative of working out our differences. Often on entering our Brethren congregation, new persons will say they find an unusually positive quality of life there. I believe this is the Christian teachings on peace that comes through. While not always popular, the positive decision for peace can affect the entire life of a congregation.

Each age calls for new voices to rise up and proclaim the timeless vision. With increasing buildups to war, re-

maining silent means we are headed backward. Preparation for war propagates war. A united witness for the way of peace is profoundly needed. If the story in this book tells us one thing, it is that the witness for peace is both needed and enduring.

The call of Jesus, the witness of others, the need for peace will help us to shape our own decision. Peacemaking can become part of our vision and commitment for what life should be when it is lived right side up. Such a stance filters down into our home, churches, school and community, where peace begins. Peace becomes a ringing call, an approach, and a solution to life's problems.

Will you give your life to this vision? A world where we study war no more? A life that will not compromise means to attain an end? Will we use the best of our minds, of our natural resources, of our human energies, of our faith to go to work for peace? Can we? Will we? Don't we have to decide for peace?

FOR PERSONAL REFLECTION AND GROUP DISCUSSION

► List ways in which one individual or group can influence another. Include as many varieties as you can from the influence of example to torture and genocide. You may want to make separate lists for individual and group actions. Include things like persuasion, spanking, war, boycott, threats, voting, television commercials, police actions, physical restraint, propaganda, withholding of friendship or of privileges, etc. Rank these in order of increasing violence. Which forms of influence are acceptable to you, if any? What kind of circumstances make a difference in your decision? What standards do you use to make your decisions?

► What recent conflicts have you been aware of and how were they solved? They could be on a national level or conflicts at home or school. What ways of handling conflicts would have been worse?

What ways better? What principles are important in dealing with conflict?

► What do you feel it would be helpful to know in order to decide your own style of being a peacemaker?

CHAPTER 2

All War Is Sin
David S. Young

The issue of war and peace became prominent again in the early 1980's when the idea of a new draft emerged. The thought of war sent a tremor down the spines of many people. On late night radio, I heard some of America's reaction to a possible registration for the draft. I was traveling across the Ohio turnpike, and President Jimmy Carter had just addressed the nation calling for a new registration. Every time I would retune my radio in order to get a stronger station, I kept picking up talk shows. The listening audience would call in their concerns and have a discussion with the radio announcer.

These talk shows were taking the pulse of a nation that had just ten years earlier experienced the heartbreak of the Vietnam war. Sleepless parents would express deep concerns about their youth being sacrificed in the useless effort of war. In most cases, the horror of war would still be heard in the voices of these parents. Why must we give up our children to such futility?

War is not only a useless effort. War is not just a needless destruction of human life. All war is sin. This is the position that the Church of the Brethren has come to about war. In 1934, the Annual Meeting of the church stated after study of the Scriptures that "we believe that war or any participation in war is wrong and incompatible with the spirit, example and teachings of Jesus Christ." This holds for all war, in any age, without exception. And it is the coming of the Son of God who has inspired the teaching of another way to live. Jesus the Christ calls us to an alternative way, different from our usual pattern of making war in order to gain or keep peace.

Let us look first of all at the man of Galilee who came upon this earth with a mission and as a model for God's way. Secondly, let us see where Jesus vigorously taught against the use of violence to solve problems. Finally, let us look at how this Man of Galilee has called us to live by conscience as followers of a way of life. In all this we will see why the Church of the Brethren, along with many other followers, concludes "All war is sin."

EVERYBODY WANTS A FRIEND

Everybody wants a friend. It's just as true when we're young as when we're old. In a friend we find a companion when we are alone; we find one who accepts us just as we are; and we find someone whose loyalty we can depend on. Friends give us a feeling of belonging, of happiness, of love. There is nothing like a friend.

When God decided to take another step to help this world, it could well be said that he chose to send a very special friend. God sent one who would accept us as we are. But this friend would also challenge us to become the best person we can be. This friend, you see, had and still has a very special mission. Just as some friends introduce us to others they know well, this friend introduces us to God. Jesus can help us to know God closely and help us to grow to become like God. This friend can have a very good influence on us.

THE MISSION OF JESUS

Perhaps this is where we can best talk about where

peace begins. Jesus had a very special mission; he came as a friend to help people come to a right relationship with God. We call this salvation. In the Old Testament it is called *shalom,* the Hebrew word meaning whole or complete or at peace. In the New Testament the word frequently used is reconciliation, which means to bring together or make as one. One verse in the Bible says God was in Christ reconciling the world to himself. It was God's hope to help people come to know him and to get along with him. It is God's hope for us to come to peace with him, and as we do that we will come to peace with ourselves and each other. Reconciliation is what Christ came to accomplish.

The way Jesus put his purpose into practice shows us the way of peace. Jesus came in a manger, not as a child of royalty. His mother waited in line outside a busy motel to find a place for him to be born. Nobody likes to wait in line, either the cafeteria line or the line behind the ticket office to the football game. Imagine that the Son of God came not as a line hopper, with privilege or status, but as one who actually was turned away when the sign read "No Vacancy." That begins to tell the story of his humble way.

He also had love and concern for people for whom no one had time. We remember the story of how Jesus was in a house and, with the press of the crowd, a sick man could not get in. When friends lowered the man through the roof, Jesus didn't scold them for ruining the roof. Rather, he had compassion and love for the sick man. He not only healed the man but also told him that his sins were forgiven. Jesus knew that healing meant bringing life together. It is the reconciliation that again is all important.

THE POWER OF LOVE

Jesus used the power of persuasive love to imple-ment his goals. He used his words rather than the sword to persuade. He turned over money tables in the temple rather than hit the people who operated the stands. He took time for children when others would disregard them. Jesus commanded his own men to put away their swords when the Roman guard came even though this cost him his own life. The bold cross speaks of one who used forgiveness in God's attempt to reunite the world.

Many said he was the Son of God. Why? Because he came to help people understand God better. Because he used love, compassion, words of truth, and deeds of service. Indeed, because he acted as people knew God would act. Christ is a friend to each person. As a friend, he can unite us with our Creator. And whereas human friends can let us down, he came as a divine friend who can help us become the person we are meant to be. Peace, then, begins as we discover this Jesus and use him as the model for our lives. He literally lived, talked, and prayed the way of peace.

MACK MODELS MEEKNESS

Christ led the early Brethren to seek an alternative to war. Alexander Mack, founder, discovered anew that the Christian life grows out of a direct relationship to Christ and to following his example. By the early 1700's, the people of Germany had experienced over fifty years of war. Alexander Mack's grandfather lived through the Thirty Years War of 1618-1648 when two Catholic armies moved over the German Palatinate, ruining all its resources. This action was followed by Protestant forces who came and burdened the people for their care.

The treaty of Westphalia that ended this war was short-lived. The Dutch war which followed almost destroyed the area in the 1670's and Alexander's father saw his town burned. Mills were ruined; fields were burned; poverty and hunger set in. The people were demoralized and persons like Mack felt the church did not care about their personal faith. Perhaps it was logical, then, for Alexander Mack to leave what he felt were only outward forms of faith in the Calvinist church. As he thought about what Christ stood for, he felt there must be some alternative to fighting. Mack and his companions had lived with enough killing. They sought to live the way of Christ instead.

THE TEACHINGS OF JESUS

Jesus not only was a model for the way of peace, he also taught the way of peace. Jesus gave short sentences to describe the ideal. "Blessed are the peacemakers, for they shall be called children of God" (Matthew 5:9). Happy are those who are not only peaceable but work continually to that peace. Then Jesus went on to describe how that life is lived. He gave the golden rule in Matthew 7:12: "Whatever you wish people to do to you, do so to them." Indeed, Jesus summed up the whole law in Matthew 22:35-40 by saying that the faithful life entails the complete love for God and unfailing love for neighbor. Peacemaking comes in constructive building of the relationships of faith and life.

Peacemaking is important also when relationships have been torn down. It was in the context of worship that Jesus calls attention to getting things right with the people around you. Jesus instructs, "if you are offering your gift at the altar, and remember that someone has something against you, leave your gift there before the altar and go; first be reconciled with them, and then come and offer your gift" (Matthew 5:23-24).

In Matthew 18, Jesus gives a way of handling differences. He instructed us to go and share with someone if we feel wronged. If that doesn't work take one or two others along and then, if necessary, let the entire church help us get together. While this passage is particularly true for people within the church, the same pattern is often used in solving conflicts at schools and in our communities. A peaceful solution—to gain the friend—is the ultimate solution. An alternative to fighting must be found. Peace is to be gained.

BOOBY TRAP BACKFIRES

A tragic illustration occurred in the summer of 1979 when a peaceful means was not used to solve a problem. A scoutmaster in Miami, Florida had his home broken into. So he decided to rig a booby trap to scare the burglar. Little did he know the consequences of his action or who would get caught. The gun used to scare the intruder went off one night when the scoutmaster was not home. As he returned, the father of one of his star scouts came running to him. His son was dead. No one knows why one of the best kids in town would have crawled through that bathroom window on that evening.

Needless to say, the scoutmaster was upset. He said that it was the first time that he had cried since Vietnam where he learned to make the booby trap. This was his comment after the experience. "Unfortunately the only thing the army taught me was how to use a weapon to destroy an individual in every possible way." The experience of killing his fourteen year old friend was almost more than he could handle. Jesus' teachings to solve one's problems peacefully comes in bold contrast to many of our solutions to human situations.

NON-RETALIATION

Perhaps the teaching of Jesus that has most influenced the Brethren is non-retaliation. This comes out of the heart of the Sermon on the Mount, Matthew 5, 6, and 7. There Jesus is addressing those who were the religious officials of that day who would have been very interested in the finer distinctions of the law. The Master begins, "You have heard it said, 'An eye for an eye and a tooth for a tooth'" (Matthew 5:38). This Old Testament law limited revenge. Restrict your revenge to what is fair, said the Old Testament. "Life for life, eye for eye, tooth for tooth, hand for hand, foot for foot" (Deuteronomy 19:21).

Jesus called for an even better way. "I say to you, Do not resist one who is evil. If anyone strikes you on the right cheek, turn the other also . . . '' (Matthew 5:39). The Jesus way is one of returning love for hate, non-resistance for evil. The person who follows Jesus does not respond in kind, but rather sets a new way of behaving. Jesus called the disciple to this better way. In the Old Testament, the law called people to be holy; in the New Testament, Jesus is calling us to be mature in love.

WHO WINS WHEN WARS WASTE WORLDS?

It takes a lot of courage not to strike back. We often hear the law of the playground used. If she hits you, hit her back. Stand up for yourself. This is the law of getting even. How many fights come about by getting even? Don't we often further antagonize when we get back at someone? Soon it becomes a battle of who is strongest and who will quit first. And who wins anyway?

What nerve and wisdom it must take not to slug back or use violent means when we are hurt or wronged. But it is by turning our cheek, by refusing to react in the same manner, that the way of peace begins. By swallowing pride and insult, we begin the process of communicating that which must occur anyway in the end. Turning our cheek is a very active, constructive way to build peace in our world. It is mature. Our behavior is directed by our beliefs rather than what others do to us. We must decide before the situation arises how we will handle conflict so that human emotions do not overtake the moment.

What is done on a personal level is also a command for the way nations should treat nations. In the same Sermon on the Mount, Jesus continued, ''You have heard it was said, 'you shall love your neighbor and hate your enemy.' But I say to you, Love your enemies and pray for those who persecute you . . . '' We don't know any law that permits hatred in the Old Testament. Jesus wanted to counter the popular way of viewing the enemy. His teaching calls us to pray for those who make life diffcult for us. The Christian way is to give active love in return for hatred.

Perhaps the summary sentence of Jesus sets the goal well. "You, therefore, must be perfect, as your heavenly Father is perfect" (Matthew 5:48). The teaching is to pattern our life after the way of God. This is a call to a mature way of life. It is a call to a courageous way of life. Indeed each individual will be challenged to live by principles that are high ideals for whatever living circumstances one is in.

SHAPING A CHRISTIAN CONSCIENCE

Besides the model of Jesus' life which conveys his mission and besides the direct teachings of Jesus on peace, we also have the call of conscience within the life of the individual Christian that puts the decision of peace before each person. By Christian conscience we mean the inner voice that speaks to us as we sensitize ourselves to what we understand to be the will of God. The statement of the Church of the Brethren on war says the church "accepts the entire New Testament as its rule of faith and practice and seeks to lead its members to comprehend and accept for themselves the mind of Christ as the guide for their convictions and conduct." So the church believes not only that all war is sin, but we also seek the right of Christian conscientious objection to all war.

When we say we are Christian *conscientious* objectors to war we mean that we have taken the life and teachings of Jesus and have let them speak to us. We feel we are being led to a position that is guided by faith. To follow conscience means to be guided like Peter who in Acts 5:29 said, "We must obey God rather than men." To follow conscience means to have heard the teachings of Paul who instructed the Romans not to do what everyone else did but to be guided by a sense of the will of God. "Do not be conformed to this world but be transformed by the renewal of your mind, that you may prove what is the will of God. What is good and acceptable and perfect" (Romans 12:2). Whereas we can see others mak-

ing different choices than our own, we seek to live by what we feel is the will of God for our own life.

Some people say that peacemaking won't work. It is difficult to believe that if you turn the other cheek the enemy won't slug you again. "Stick up for yourself" is a generally agreed upon rule. We hear "No one else will stick up for you." It is by conscience that we will need to meet both those arguments. Whether it will work is an important question. But a more important question is, "What is right?" It will be by conscience that we will get the courage to meet the situations where we may be slugged back. In fact, conscience becomes that guiding force that leads us through life. Seeking the mind of Christ in each circumstance distinguishes us as followers of Christ's way.

It was a call of conscience that led a group of young people at the 1948 Annual Conference of the Church of the Brethren to do what was almost an unprecedented action. The youth presented the 162nd recorded conference with a new item of business. They presented a plea for a plan that would put into action the general statement of the conference on the sin of war. They also recommended that a broad plan of volunteer service be implemented. This group of youth, moved by conscience, led the church in creating a form of alternative service known as Brethren Volunteer Service. Youth have since worked in projects around the world in order to live the way of peace.

ALL WAR IS SIN

All war is sin. Fighting stands in contradiction to the model Jesus lived with the mission he was on; fighting stands in contradiction to the teachings of Christ in the Gospel for the way of life that is fulfilling. Increasingly persons of conscience are saying that fighting stands in contradiction to what is right. The way of peace finally trusts in God to bring his world together in his way.

It all becomes very personal, then. We are deciding

the ideal by which to live our lives in very practical situations. We believe all war is sin. Peacemaking is a positive, constructive use of one's life. It calls for a use of
one's life that builds toward the unity we know God in-
tends.

The final purpose of our teachings on peace is well
stated in the Annual Conference statement, "We seek
thereby to lead individuals into such intimate contact
with Jesus Christ, our Lord, that they will commit themselves to him and to the manner of life which he taught
and exemplified." We are each invited by the Master to
follow him.

FOR REFLECTION AND DISCUSSION

► The story of the scoutmaster (page 13) shows the
   problems one might meet while trying to defend
   one's property. What other methods might the
   scoutmaster have used? What would be a New
   Testament approach to property and its defense?

► With the aid of a concordance, make a list of
   passages in the Bible that deal with peace. You
   may discover some which do not sound as "peaceful" as others. Although our understanding of
   Jesus is based on the total picture, not individual
   passages, how do you explain the presence of the
   less peaceful passages?

► The motto of the Strategic Air Command is "Peace
   is Our Profession." The Brethren declare "All War
   is Sin." Do these two agree in their goals? In their
   methods? What problems and differences do you
   see between these two groups?

► What role does anger have in the life of a Christian? When is it alright to be angry? What do you
   do when angry?

CHAPTER 3

Brethren Peacemakers
Joan Deeter

Why would a soft spoken young Brethren mother break the law, committing an act that she knew would lead to her arrest, trial, and conviction? Jean Warstler Zimmerman chose to protest at a nuclear plant in Rocky Flats, Colorado because she believed what they were doing there threatened the lives of children, including her daughters, Kristi and Lori.

Jean was one of nine who worshipped together on the tracks leading into the plant. They continued to sing and pray in an area forbidden to outsiders, knowing their arrest was likely. Jean explains, "It was important for me to go to the tracks and not just talk." Further tying the action to her church roots, Jean continues, "I had learned Brethren principles of pacifism in my home life. . . . I knew I had children and I had to be involved. For me the protest was Church of the Brethren related."

Jean was arrested and with others used the trial as another opportunity to call attention not only to the horrors of nuclear war, but also to the serious danger in the plant itself. Many experts came to testify about the way radiation damages health. None of them were given a chance to speak. Jean was allowed to make her witness in court. "When I was on the stand," she reports, "I felt they were trying the next generation. They're going to have to fight for the right to live on this planet."

After nine hours, Jean heard the verdict. Her sentence was six months' unsupervised probation. Jean was able to return home with her family and continue her witness for peace. She frequently speaks and leads seminars with youth and adults. Aware of the special burden young people carry, Jean told a youth session at the 1980 Annual Conference, "When young persons are little, adults get angry if they refuse to fight. We ask young people to fight older people's conflicts."

Jean remembers, "When I was a teenager I escaped the issue because I was a girl. The problem belongs to all of us and I want to share it and witness." This Jean clearly continues to do, constantly seeking fresh ways to speak out for peace.

In 1979 the Atlantic Northeast District Brethren Peace Fellowship gave Jean the Brethren Peacemaker of the Year Award. Their statement concludes, "You have stirred us all to care more and do more."

Jean follows in a long tradition of Brethren witnesses against war. Andrew Boni may have been the first. He was one of the first 8 to be baptized in Schwarzenau in 1708. Earlier he had been arrested several times and expelled from Basel, Switzerland, in part because he refused to wear the customary side arms.

JOHN KLINE

Through the years the Brethren have remembered and honored the church's outstanding witnesses for peace. One favorite story is that of Elder John Kline. Mostly on horseback he covered 100,000 miles, preaching in churches, visiting in the homes to aid the sick and encourage those who struggled with personal or spiritual problems. Even Kline's horse, Nell, has become well known for having covered most of those miles with him. John Kline showed the warmth of his spirit in the way he spoke of the mare. He recalled Martin Luther and John Wesley had earlier expressed a view that there might be a special heavenly provision for animals. "But, as we have no assurance of this," he says, "I desire to reward her in this world as well as I can for her gentle, untiring service."

He reported that Nell "not only had her favorite places to stop at, but she had her favorite roads to travel on. And it was not uncommon for her rider to be forced into a mild but resolute contention with her when he wished to leave a road he had repeatedly traveled before."

JOHN KLINE FIGHTS DISEASE, NOT PEOPLE

Often John Kline had the sad duty of conducting the funerals of persons whom the medicine of his day was unable to save. Comments in his diary show how deeply he felt the pain of families' grief, particularly over the deaths of young children. John and Anna Kline's only child had been born dead.

In the diary Kline tells about two families that each buried three young children within a month's time. In 1862 he conducted 56 funerals and 32 of those were children under 10 years old. One feels John Kline's sharing of sadness with the parents and also his strong faith that there was hope for a future reunion.

However, he not only offered sympathy, he also fought disease. Even though he spent very little time in school, John Kline read a lot, particularly studying the Bible and medicine. Treating the sick, he rejected some of the earlier practices such as bleeding or starving patients. He made use of herbs and plant leaves he gathered in the woods as part of a course of treatment.

The most difficult disease with which John Kline struggled was the mental illness of his wife, Anna. She became severely depressed when she received news from Ohio that he was near death there. He returned home well, but she never fully recovered. He tried every treatment he knew, including electric shock, but nothing

worked. Relatives moved into their home to be with her
so that Kline could continue his leadership in the church.

PEACEMAKER KLINE

John Kline proved he was a peacemaker on a personal level when he went to visit a friend and frequent
opponent, Joseph Funk. In his diary in October 1862
Kline reports he "succeed(ed) in bringing about a better
state of feeling on his part toward me. He became reconciled." They ate a meal together before Kline returned
home. Since Funk died two months later, that peace became the last chapter in their often difficult relationship.

Throughout his ministry John Kline described the
way he thought Christians should live. In a sermon in
1845, nearly twenty years before the Civil War, he described the bearing of arms, military service, as the greatest of all earthly evils.

Two years later on the 4th of July in 1847, after hearing of a North Carolina slave sale that separated a
mother and her three children under twelve, he wrote in
his diary, "I do believe that the time is not far distant
when the sun will rise and set upon our land cleansed of
this foul stain, though it may be cleansed with blood. I
would rejoice to think that my eyes might see that bright
morning, but I can have no hope of that."

We remember John Kline best for his work for the
church during the Civil War. Brethren in the south had
an especially difficult time because they had been pub-
licly against slavery and separation from the union.
They were, therefore, suspected of being traitors.
Added to this was the great need the south had for
men to fight.

Kline, as a leader, became well known not only for
his opinions, but also his actions. He encouraged young
men not to become soldiers and worked hard to get the
government to recognize the peace position of the
church. It was no way to win a popularity contest.

PEACEMAKING CAN BE HAZARDOUS

John Kline, with others, was finally successful in getting a law passed that recognized some young men could not fight because of the teachings of their church. After paying a sum of money they were excused. Some were arrested first and John Kline himself was also put into prison. Virginia was facing an invasion by northern forces and it is possible the officials were not sure these Brethren and Mennonite pacifists could be trusted.

After the release John Kline continued to take leadership in presenting the concerns of the Brethren to the government. He believed it was so important that they remain faithful to their peace beliefs that if necessary they should ask permission to leave with or without their property.

Another risk John Kline took during the Civil War years was the annual journey to the north to serve as moderator of the Conference. He was certainly aware of the danger involved in making these trips. On May 19, 1864, following the Annual Conference near Hagerstown, Indiana, John Kline told a group of Brethren, "Possibly you may never see my face or hear my voice again. I am now on my way back to Virginia, not knowing the things that shall befall me there. It may be that bonds or afflictions abide me. But I feel that I have done nothing worthy of bonds or of death; and none of these things move me; neither count I my life dear unto myself, so that I may finish my course with joy, and the ministry which I have received of the Lord Jesus to testify the Gospel of the grace of God."

He arrived home safely from conference, but in a June 13 letter he reported, "Times are squally here now." The Northern Army was advancing once more. Showing his concern for all persons, John Kline concluded with a prayer that God "will so interfere that this awful and unnecessary war might be closed, and peace and amity restored."

"NEVER SHRINK FROM THE CALL OF DUTY"

Once more on June 14 he was warned by a friend that he was in danger and that he should be careful in his travels. To this John Kline's reply was that he "hoped he should never shrink from the call of duty, wherever the summons might lead him."

The next day he was ambushed by two local Confederate soldiers. The first shot entered his back, but after he had fallen, the attacker moved forward and fired again into his chest. Since neither his money nor his watch were taken, it was obvious robbery was not the motive for the killing.

John Kline had been known and loved by the Brethren during a long ministry. The shot that ended his life stamped his name firmly in the pages of Brethren history. He was not able to stop the war from coming, nor end it after it started, but no threat stopped him from living each day directed by his faith and concern for people.

His witness for peace was present in a total life that served others.

In time of war Brethren witness for peace and against war. In peacetime also there have been Brethren who have given their lives to solving the problems that lead to war. Two of these persons have made a witness that has touched people around the world.

DAN WEST

Dan West was born on a farm in southern Ohio. Strongly rooted in the Church of the Brethren, Dan began his active peace witness when he was drafted for World War I. He had decided he could train, carry a mess kit, even salute. Then one day his group was asked, "Anyone here who objects to fighting for the cause of the Allies?" Dan replied, "Yes." He talked with the sergeant, trying to explain his conscientious objection, but he found his name on a list for a machine gun battalion. Dan faced curses and taunts when he refused to go, but he had decided he would rather go to Leavenworth Prison than act against his conscience. Instead, after a time, the Army released him.

Throughout his life, Dan focused on young people. He did whatever he could to make them start thinking seriously about peacemaking. He said, "When I see so much war makers are doing and so little that peacemakers are doing, I wonder why the difference. Find me one hundred young persons between the ages of twenty-one and thirty who will give as much for peace as a soldier gives for war, and we will change the thinking of Congress in three years' time."

In her book on Dan West, *Passing on the Gift,* Glee Yoder suggests that like an itinerant Johnny Appleseed he moved about spreading the seeds of goodwill and peace.

COWBOY DAN

Dan not only pushed others to think about ways to

work for peace, he never stopped thinking himself. In the winter of 1937-38 Dan worked to feed Spanish children dying of hunger because of the civil war that tore that country apart. Since there was not enough milk available for all who needed it, those babies that did not gain weight were no longer given any. Dan suffered greatly when he had to carry out decisions that he knew would lead to death for the weakest children.

Haunted by the faces of dying children, Dan began to dream of some way to provide more milk. Out of his personal pain was born the vision of giving animals to families in need. Dan reasoned it made sense to make a gift of a cow that could furnish milk for years. An additional part of his plan was to require all those who received gift animals to pass the first female offspring on to another family. In this way, those who received had the opportunity to have the satisfaction and self respect that comes in being able to give.

Other persons helped to translate Dan's dream into a program. Six years later the first eighteen heifers were sent to Puerto Rico. Two of those animals were still producing 2456 pounds of milk a month eleven years later, clear evidence of the wisdom of Dan's idea. The Heifer Project International, born from Dan's vision, has now placed over 50,000 animals and over 1½ million chickens with persons in need in over ninety countries and more than twenty states in the USA. It has also provided many persons a direct contact with those in need. Farmers, doctors, clergy, teachers, young and old, men and women, served as "cowboys," accompanying the animal gifts to their destinations.

NEITHER CAKE NOR GAVEL

Dan's life was ruled by his belief that the way to bring peace was by tackling the problems that could lead to war. He was serious about being a brother to every person alive. Many remember his saying, "I will not eat cake when others in the world do not have bread." When he

was moderator of Annual Conference in 1966, he lifted a
towel rather than a gavel as a reminder of the Brethren
feetwashing, symbol of service. The difficulty he sometimes found in shouldering the weight of constant concern for peace and the needs of persons is expressed in a
poem he wrote in *Messenger* in 1967. He titled it *Which
Cross?*

> Dear Lord, my cross is heavy. The weight of it—
> With other things—is bending down my head.
> My knees are weak . . . My back and arms are sore.
> Do I have to carry it anymore?
> Couldn't I just worship yours instead?

Four years later, unable to speak, spending his final
months in a nursing home, Dan West still wrote notes to
family and visitors, raising questions, making sugges-
tions. He never stopped caring or working with his mind
at the problems that had been at the center of his life.

M. R. ZIGLER

Working with Dan for many years was another outstanding Brethren peace leader, Michael Robert Zigler,
who wrote Chapter 8 of this handbook. M. R. has never
wanted Brethren to become too comfortable about what
they are doing for peace. He may applaud good ideas,
but not as a stopping point. M. R. keeps talking and
pushing people to take action. Andy Murray's song,
Work, Don't Weep, which Andy dedicated to M. R. when
he introduced it at the 1977 Annual Conference in Rich-
mond, Virginia, catches that special spirit.

Through many decades M. R. has shared his vision
that a world of peace is possible and that Brethren need
to be busy taking the lead to make it happen. M. R.
helped to create and carry out Brethren programs to
serve the victims of war. He was one of those who
formed and won government acceptance for a World
War II alternative service program that gave drafted
men a choice.

In the larger church family, the World Council of

Churches, M. R. pushed the Brethren concern for a church, serving the needs of people and condemning war.

After retirement, over 80, M. R. began once again to push a dream, <u>On Earth Peace</u>. It was a new effort by Brethren to find a road to peace for everyone. Talking to one group he had called together to work on the project, M. R. promised with a twinkle in his eye, "If you young guys don't keep working for peace when I die, I'll come back from the grave and haunt you."

TED STUDEBAKER

Through the years Brethren have been stirred by the many young men who have refused to fight. One of these was Ted Studebaker. On April 25, 1971, Ted Studebaker died in Vietnam. He did not wear a uniform or carry a gun. He worked for Vietnam Christian Service.

Like many others his age, Ted grew up working on the

family farm, enjoying sports, music, and friends. Responding to the tragedy of Vietnam, Ted went there, lived among people, learned their language, worked with them to improve life in the villages. He felt strongly about being a Christian Service volunteer rather than a soldier. He talked about it in letters to friends.

> Without the church. . . . I might find myself in uniform as part of a giant military machine. . . . I believe strongly in trying to follow the example of Jesus Christ as best I know how. Above all, Christ taught me to love all people, including enemies, and to return good for evil, and that all men are my brothers in Christ. I condemn all war and conscientiously refuse to take part in it in any active or violent way. I believe love is a stronger and more enduring power than hatred for all my fellowmen, regardless of who they are or what they believe.

Ted, recently married when he was killed, felt great satisfaction in the choices he had made. The strength of that feeling is obvious in a letter he wrote hours before he was killed. "I know I am a fortunate man and life is great to me."

His bride of one week, Ven Pak Studebaker, wanting to underscore the message of Ted's life, asked friends after his death to not only grieve for Ted, but "grieve even more for those who do not understand what he did."

THE LIST GOES ON

The number of Brethren peace witnesses continues to grow. Every day a new story is added. There are Brethren all over the world committed to the vision of peace on this planet. Because they value human life, they tackle problems like pain, unemployment, injustice, and hunger. Believing all war is wrong, they protest against all the nation's military activities and expenditures. They resist, even at the risk of arrest, being an active part of the defense system.

As a church together we work for peace wherever there is an opportunity. Persons are hired to work at peace in special ways—at the United Nations, in Washington, D.C., through education, with other groups and churches. Because young people with the help of Dan West convinced the 1948 Annual Conference it was important, we have Brethren Volunteer Service. Through it more than 4,000 volunteers, ages 18-75, have served persons in need around the world. Stories could be written about each of them or those others who have served through Brethren Service or in their local community through the newer Parish Volunteer Service.

Stories could be told about many other witnesses to peace. The list could fill this book. It should include every member of the Church of the Brethren. In our lives are written the stories others will read for peace.

FOR CONSIDERATION

▶ As a group, listen to some of the following songs of Andy Murray:
"The Ballad of John Kline" and "Cowboy Dan" from the record *Summertime Children,* Church of the Brethren, 1975; and "Work, Don't Weep" and "Brave Man From Ohio" from the record *Goodbye Still Night,* Brethren Press, 1978.

▶ Have group members find the stories of persons mentioned and others in *Messenger* and share them with the class.

▶ Identify "peace witnesses" known to the group.

CHAPTER 4

Peaceful Youth Programs
James E. Miller

Laughter and excitement poured out the doors of our church's fellowship hall when Shannon walked in. The Junior High Fellowship was getting started that Sunday evening. Inside the room, the youth were ready for a fun game of Lap Ball. Shannon hurried over to the circle and sat down on the floor beside Ngong, one of the Vietnamese in our church.

Lap Ball was fun! There were ten youth and advisors with our feet all touching in the center of the circle, legs outstretched and hands on the floor behind our backs, supporting our bodies. The volleyball quickly moved from lap to lap. Occasionally it got stuck near someone's ankles and getting it started brought out the clowning genius in the two working together. It takes a lot of cooperation to pass the ball to the next person and not let it fall between your legs.

The evening continued with sharing clusters working on the Sermon on the Mount. Jesus' teachings had a way of coming alive as Nancy led the group in Bible Study. Four youth in each cluster had a chance to think for themselves and then share what Jesus' teachings meant then and now. Shannon talked about how it felt when

Jerry had insulted him because he felt they should include Ngong on their school soccer team.

What did Jesus' disciples really think he meant when he said we are to love our enemy? "Have you seen my 'enemy list' recently? You don't just say 'Peace!' to them! It's so much easier to go the other way," Shannon shared. Well, anyway, that's why the clusters are so good. It's a place and a time to study and share with each other. We don't all agree and we don't all have to agree. Nancy keeps reminding us that no one has yet figured out *all* the answers. It really is more important to know why we think as we do—and to know what the Bible and our church leaders have thought through.

SERIOUS FUN

Peace Education is fun and it touches many different parts of Shannon's youth group. It is fun when cooperative games are played. It is serious when Bible Study and sharing take place. It is learning how to plan and work together. And it is no accident. Fred and Nancy are youth counselors who take seriously their work with the junior highs. With their pastor, they have carefully built peace education, cooperative games, study of the Bible, and church history into a popular, well attended youth program. They are committed to this approach. They do not only believe that someday these youth will lead the church, but that right *now* they are the church. They are youth easily influenced by the TV and popular school attitudes that "might is right," "our country must be number one," "the Army is the way to better jobs," etc.

A solid base where strong relationships develop and people matter, where differing views are accepted and tested, and where peace becomes a live option are some of the goals of Fred and Nancy. Let's get back to Shannon telling about that youth group.

TELLING THE PEACEMAKING STORY

After the small groups were finished, it was time to

get back in the larger group where Fred had set up the projector and screen. About a month ago, M. R. Zigler came to our church to talk about peace. Before worship, we had a time for youth and adults to meet. M. R. Zigler had the youth sit in a small circle near him. Their grandparents sat in a circle behind the youth and children. Our parents had to sit in the back. We learned a bit about what our church is doing to bring peace alive. There are older youth and adults working in hospitals in countries where food and water shortages make many sick. There are other Brethren teaching children to read and count and plant gardens or raise goats. It is really a way of living. Peace is not only saying, "I'm *not* going into the military," but it is also saying, "I *am* going to live for others—do something different, like work for peace."

Since then, our junior high group has been making a slide/tape show telling the peacemaking story of our own church. Our advisors and pastor have helped us meet several people in our church who have done something

to make peace on earth a little more real. Our work tonight is to see the pictures and begin putting together a sound track from the taped interviews and music some of our group performed. Several in our group made pictures and posters for the title and credit slides.

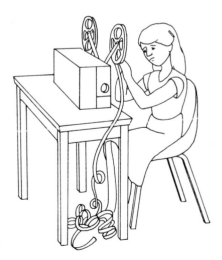

Others were good at interviewing people. Tom found out that his great uncle had gone to jail back in 1941 when there was a war because he would not cooperate by being drafted for the Army. He said he would rather follow Jesus' word that we are to love our enemies. It seemed to him that military service just didn't fit.

Sharon learned that the family of her good friend, Mary Togasaki, had been helped when Japanese-Americans had been sent to concentration camps in the United States during World War II. Her uncle had lived a while in a Brethren Hostel in Chicago at a time when love for the enemy was hard to explain to your neighbors who only saw the Togasakis as "Japs."

There is a lot of work still to be done on our slide/tape show, but that will wait till next week. Now, it is time for popcorn and apples.

A PEACE DAISY

For our closing worship, Nancy and Fred had set up a giant daisy. Its green stem and leaves were made of poster paper with scriptures speaking about love of enemy, going the second mile, and who is my neighbor? Other scriptures made it clear how hard it is to actually do what Jesus asks: count the cost; walk the second mile; turn the other cheek; if you are cursed and rebuked for my sake . . .

Our youth group had been building this peace daisy for several months. We knew it needed a strong base in Jesus' teachings if it was ever to stand up. On the grassy base these scriptures were printed:

Love your enemies, do good to those who hate you, bless those who curse you, pray for those who abuse you. To him who strikes you on the cheek, offer the other also.

(Luke 6:27, 28)

So whatever you wish that men would do to you, do so to them; for this is the law and the prophets.

(Matthew 7:12)

Put your sword back into its place; for all who take the sword will perish by the sword.

(Matthew 26:52)

Tonight Nancy placed a tight bud on the top of the stem. We were curious what this would lead to. Fred handed out a paper that he said would be our game plan for the next several weeks. Its title was "What does our church say about war and peace?"

WHAT DOES OUR CHURCH SAY ABOUT WAR AND PEACE?

The Church of the Brethren regards with sorrow and deep concern our nation's increasing movement toward a permanently militaristic outlook. Two devastating world wars, the conflict in Korea, the Vietnam War, and the many international crises of recent decades have produced an alarming change in American attitudes toward war and peace. The American public may come to accept as normal and inevitable the prospect that the nation must be prepared to go to war at any moment, that every young man must spend time in military service, that an overwhelming share of our heavy federal taxes must be devoted to military needs, and that this country must always be willing to assume the military burdens of weaker allies, actual or potential.

Because of our complete dissent from these assumptions, the Church of the Brethren desires again, as at other times in its history, to declare its convictions about war and peace, military service and conscriptions, the use of tax money for military purposes, the right of Christian conscience, and the responsibility of Christian citizenship . . .

The official position of the Church of the Brethren is that all war is sin and that we seek the right of conscientious objection to all war. We seek no special privileges from our government. What we seek for ourselves, we seek for all — the right of individual conscience. We affirm that this conscientious objection may include all wars, declared or undeclared; particular wars; and particular forms of warfare. We also affirm that conscientious objection may be based on grounds more inclusive than institutional religion.

The Church of the Brethren, since its beginning in 1708, has repeatedly declared its position against war. Our understanding of the life and the teaching of Christ, as revealed in the New Testament, led our Annual Conference to state in 1785 that we should not "submit to the higher powers so as to make ourselves their instruments to shed human blood." In 1918, at our Annual Conference, we stated that "we believe that war or any participation in war is wrong and incompatible with the spirit, example, and teachings of Jesus Christ." Again in 1934, Annual Conference resolved that "all war is sin. We, therefore, cannot encourage, engage in, or willingly profit from armed conflict at home, or abroad. We cannot, in the event of war, accept military service or support the military machine in any capacity."
(From "A Statement of the Church of the Brethren on War." 1970 Annual Conference)

As we study our Church of the Brethren Statement on War, Fred said we would see the bud unfold. We will also be thinking about our own response. Each petal had a different name of a person in our group. As we felt led, we would share our own peace plans for our lives. In that way, our stories will become the flower on the peace daisy.

ACTIVITIES HELPING YOUTH LEARN ABOUT PEACE

If you felt you would like to be a part of Shannon's youth group with Fred and Nancy as your advisors, you are not alone. This story is taken from real youth groups in Churches of the Brethren.

For a few weeks each year, there are specific studies on peace, Brethren history, and news articles about current peace activities. This fits part of the total program of the leaders to broaden the horizon of the group. They explored their faith, their relationships with one another, and their own self understanding.

Peace studies is not the full story of the youth group. There were good times at swimming parties and hayrides. There were overnight retreats with the pastor for those interested in baptism and church membership. Interesting speakers dropped in to talk about many aspects of the life of the youth, such as sports and Christian living, recycling aluminum cans, and getting along in a home with one parent.

How can your youth group learn about peace? Other chapters in this book provide the content related to Bible study, Brethren history, and current issues facing youth. This chapter is planned to give you some ideas to use in your youth group that teach peace. We all need a vehicle that matches our transportation needs. As students, we need a plan for peace education that is itself an experiment in peace living.

The activities given earlier of Shannon's youth group sound like fun. There is also a purpose behind them. Let's look at some of the ways those activities help us think about peace living and peacemaking.

- Learning about peace living is part of learning about Jesus and our church. As so is service, caring for a hungry world, being conservers of energy as well as trying to live like Jesus' disciples and finding a deep sense of God's love for us. That is to say, peace is not an elective, nor is it a special, separate interest. It is a part of everything.

- No matter what age we are, peace education fits our interests and concerns. As youth, we have special interests and ideas about peace that the rest of the church needs to hear.

- We are working for a clear sense of what's worth living for. Our advisors will have a sense of what is most important to them, and so do our parents, teachers, and pastor. Even in our group, we probably will have different ideas. That's O.K. What's really important is

learning why my values are *mine*. In this way, I will listen openly to others' ideas and find belief that suits me in a changing and challenging world.
• The community and church recognize youth as citizens and leaders in the twenty-first century. We are called to a deeper sense of being Jesus' followers, and this will lead us as we discover new insights and find new resources to meet life's conflicts nonviolently.

DESIGNING A PROGRAM

What can be taken from this chapter to your youth group? Here is a way to use the game described at the beginning of this chapter as a learning event. Let's call this youth program: "Violence and Nonviolence: The Games We Play."

Purpose Our own behavior and attitudes, informal and recreational activities, can help us explore the issue of competition and cooperation/violence and nonviolence..

Background Competition and cooperation are basic attitudes that make up our "lifestyle." This is one way of exploring the Biblical theme of *shalom* (peace). If we believe nonviolence is a better way to settle political conflicts, is it not also a better way to live all our social relationships, including the games we play? (I Thessalonians 5:23).

Preparation Needed Hang pieces of hard candy by string from the ceiling of the room. These should be about twelve inches over the heads of the tallest person. Use only one piece of candy for each three students.

Teaching Plans Begin by asking each person to list the games they have played in the last month. Then ask them to decide which emphasized competition and which encouraged cooperation.

Now divide the group into teams of three. One by one, have each team go to an area where the candy is hanging. The group of three are told they can have one piece of candy if they can get it down without touching the string or the candy with their hands. They will soon discover that the only way to get the candy is for two team members to lift the third and the third one take the candy by mouth. After taking the candy in the mouth, the only thing for that person to do is to eat the candy, and the other two to do without. There is only enough candy for one piece for each group.

Immediately after playing this game, have the group play lap ball as described in the first part of this chapter.

When you are through playing lap ball, have the group re-form for discussion. On a piece of scratch paper have each person rank answers to the following question: Which do you think best expresses peacemaking in the games we play and in our living?

☐ Let's get together and figure out what went wrong.

☐ I told you so, but let's forget it.

☐ I'll be here if you need me.

☐ What you do doesn't matter to me.

After all have marked their papers have them stand up and place themselves on an imaginary continuum across the room. The question for them to respond to is: "How necessary are wars?" On one side of the room the extreme would be, "We will always have wars because people are greedy and like to fight." On the other extreme of the room would be those who say, "We can use our minds and find ways to settle differences peacefully." Note that this is a continuum in which there are many points between the two extremes. Have them move quickly to that part of the room where they feel most comfortable in answering the question.

After the games have been played and the value

clarification exercises completed, allow time for everyone to respond. The following questions might help them
begin: "What were the differences in the games?"
"Which did you most enjoy? Why?" "What kinds of
players are needed in each game for it to be successful?"
It has been found that after this kind of a discussion,
even those who lost the candy in the first game can share
questions like "Who really got the greatest prize in that
game?"

One way to pull the whole evening together is a
period of worship. Use this worship situation for sharing
about the events of the evening and insights persons
have found. Reading scriptures such as Ephesians 6:10-20
along with a closing song would make a suitable closing
worship.

The opportunity is now yours for finding ways of
building a youth program for peace. This discussion
guide and the examples from youth groups are a spring-
board for your own youth group. One way to get going is
to bring persons together to brainstorm on opportunities
that can work now in your group. It is also helpful to find
one concrete example of peace education that you can
commit yourself to trying in your own church.

CHAPTER 5

World Peacemaking
Ruby F. Rhoades

What kind of situation brings you to the point of saying "That makes me so mad I could hit somebody"? Let me make some guesses.

Someone messes up something that belongs to you, wrecks your bike or breaks your tennis racket, or worse yet, breaks up your relationship with your best friend. Or maybe it's when you see someone take advantage of another person, like taking a ball away from a little kid or being rude and even mean to a person who can't speak English or who is different in some way. Maybe it's when your little brother or sister comes home crying because some bigger kids chased the younger ones off the playground. Or is it when someone runs a red light just as you're crossing the street on green—and no one else sees or does anything about it?

Do you ever feel angry when you hear talk about the use of our world's resources and you're not sure there'll be any left for your generation or for your children? Yet you're helpless to do anything about it. Do you ever feel frustrated because what you learn in church school class about turning the other cheek and loving your enemies seems good advice only for personal relationships but not very practical in international affairs?

We'll not talk about how you deal with anger and frustration in this chapter. What we want to note here is that the same such frustrations, when multiplied many times over, become the basis for international disputes —and even for armed wars. We're going to look at four topics in this chapter: what makes for war, what makes for peace, how Brethren are working at peacemaking, and what *you* can do.

WHAT MAKES FOR WAR

Basically wars happen because we fail to obey God's laws of loving, forgiving and seeking justice for all people. But we probably need to look at specifics in order to understand what that means in our world today. So let's take a look.

Human rights   We all have an idea of what human rights are—especially when it comes to our own. I'll mention some and you be thinking of others: the right to free speech, the freedom to worship as we choose, the right to speak out about our government when we feel it does something wrong, the right to privacy, equality, the right to object to bearing arms and to oppose war in general. What other rights do you believe are yours?

In some countries around the world, we would hear other responses to that question. Some would say they have the human right to food, to health care, to a place to live, to work, to education, to freedom from the fear of arbitrary arrest, and to freedom from torture. Did you think of any of these? If so, why or why not? We may not have thought of them because we've always had them. But many people in the world are victims of torture, discrimination, poor health, illiteracy, malnutrition, and other inhuman treatment. They become angry, with reason, demand their rights and are ready to fight, and die if necessary, to get what they believe belongs to them as human beings.

We need to remember that *certain* rights like electing our leaders are ours because of a democratic government but that the real *rights of persons* are derived from God's law which teaches accountability to God, to neighbor and to ourselves. Look up Matthew 22:37-40. What does it mean to love in this way, to feel and make others feel loved and totally a human being? How far would you go to protect those things that contribute to "humanness"? Would you fight for these rights for yourself? Harder yet, what would you be willing to sacrifice to see that *others* have these rights?

Economic injustice Could you give a very simple definition of what you think economic injustice is? Let me try several. It's the situation that exists when for a few persons to have a lot, the majority must have little or nothing. Or it is when the powerful nations of the world shape the patterns and terms of trade to their own economic advantage. Or—it's what happens when profit becomes more important than people. And probably it's all three.

Many policies of our big business companies, multinational or transnational they're called, are examples of what I'm talking about. Because the people of the United States can afford to pay the price, we'll be supplied with tomatoes, strawberries and pineapples for our tables all year. But precious land is being used in countries where people are hungry in order to satisfy our tastes—because it's *profitable* to the companies importing the special foods. Corporation policies usually don't care about the people, whether in Mexico or Sri Lanka or El Salvador—they want the product that will bring the highest profits.

Some of you may have stopped eating Nestlé chocolate. Our boycott of that company is one way to work at correcting economic injustice. Let me explain about that boycott. As the population in the United States has leveled off, the market for baby formula also leveled off.

That's understandable. When business feels such a pinch, however, it seeks new markets for its products.

Nestlé did just that and chose Third World mothers as its new target market. The company found powerful ways to persuade those mothers to use their powdered baby formula. Only many women can't read the directions on the tins; they don't know they must boil the water and sterlize the bottles. If they don't have enough powder, they use less, just so it "looks white." Babies develop diarrhea, they dehydrate, are malnourished and dying, but the important thing for the Nestlé company is to make a profit.

This kind of exploitation is wrong. The Old Testament prophets got very angry when they saw such injustice and warned the people of coming punishment for such actions. You may want to look up some scriptures that talk about economic injustice: Is. 10:1-4, Amos 4:1-2; 8:4-6, Luke 1:46-53, 6:20-25, James 5:3-5.

Arms race Over a billion dollars a day are being spent in our world on the arms race. There are over a billion people suffering malnutrition every day. Could there be a connection? Even as we continue with our research and production of ever more accurate weapons, we are already able to destroy the world many times over. The Soviet Union has roughly the same abilities for destruction. As we perfect our weapons systems, they also perfect theirs. Each of us annually increases our military spending and we both call it *national security.*

The weapons that are being produced are more accurate and more devastating than ever. Now we have developed a bomb called the *neutron bomb.* This bomb doesn't destroy buildings and property, it only kills *people.* The death it inflicts is a slow, terribly painful one. The United States is the first to develop this deadly weapon, but others will soon follow.

Today the United States' nuclear arsenal contains at least 35,000 nuclear warheads. The world total is about twice that number. More countries are testing and researching nuclear weapons; six countries are known to have them, at least 15 others are in a "near-nuclear" status. This is called *nuclear proliferation* and is a strong threat to world peace.

Someone said to me, "We shouldn't frighten people, especially the young people." I believe you should be scared, so scared you'll start asking, "What can I do?" and then do something about it. It's *your* future!

WHAT MAKES FOR WORLD PEACE?

We have looked at some causes of war, now let's think about what makes for peace in our world.

Disarmament This is not a popular word today. Most people prefer "superiority" or even "parity" (find out what the word means) and are frightened to think of actually disarming or getting rid of any of our weapons.

Our country was the first to test nuclear weapons; the first and only country to actually use them in war. We've been the first to develop many new kinds of weapons, the neutron bomb for instance, and we're first in weapons sales to other countries. Some record! We have contributed heavily to the arming of the entire world. Isn't it time we take the first faith step in disarming the world by beginning with our own overstocked arsenal?

Until one of the superpowers (the United States or the Soviet Union) is willing to begin the dismantling process, we will all be caught in a race nobody can win. The first step would be to prohibit any further nuclear explosions. Then all weapons research and production should be immediately halted and we should move into dismantling what we already have. We could begin this process by making agreements with the Soviet Union jointly and by simultaneously setting limits on production. This could be a treaty such as the SALT II treaty which our country has not even been willing to sign (as of

this writing). Disarmament is a step-by-step process, and
we must be willing to take the first step.

National Security   It is assumed by many people
that we are safer because we are protected by such a
"strong" weapons system and because we are the
Number One power in the world. Do you feel more
secure? I don't. If my neighbor is mad at me about
something, I'd sure rather know that neither of us is
bringing a gun to work it out. As long as our country continues to pile up deadly weapons, our security is
lessened. How do you feel about this security? What
makes you feel safe?

Conflict resolution   There are alternatives for working at
conflict. More effective communication is one. Talking
together about problems and disagreements can often
result in a satisfactory agreement. The use of international bodies, such as the United Nations, for settling
disputes is another way.

As Christians, we are called to be peacemakers.
We're also taught how to treat our "enemies" and work
out our problems. Can you think of ways to influence our
government to work at conflict resolution instead of
arms production?

A more just society   Working for a more just society
is another way toward peace in our world. Just as
injustice or suffering sows the seeds for war making, so does justice and right doing pave the way for
peace.

Look back again at the things that make you and me
angry. Translate those situations into an international
scale—big powerful countries exploiting smaller ones;
strong, well-armed countries controlling weaker, de-
fenseless ones; the rich taking from the poor. If *you*
almost come to the point of hitting someone, can you
understand why nations rise up in anger?

THE CHURCH OF THE BRETHREN WORKS AT PEACEMAKING

We can be very proud of our church's concern and actions for world peace. You have already read about some of the peacemakers in our heritage. Our efforts continue in many ways.

Persons working at peace issues The Church of the Brethren employs four persons to work continuously on peace issues. One, the Peace Education Consultant, conducts workshops and counsels youth on registration and draft issues. A second, the Peace/International Affairs Consultant, works with international groups around the world in Ireland, the Middle East, the Soviet Union, for instance, trying to find ways to bring reconciliation. The third is our Washington Office Representative who works on peace and justice issues in relation to public policy, witnesses to government, and keeps our members informed about issues before Congress. Since 1978, we have also had a representative at the United Nations, carrying our peace witness into meetings and discussions with persons from all around the world. These four persons make up the *Peace Team* and work together on special peace emphases for our church.

New Call to Peacemaking Early in 1977, the three historic peace churches, Church of the Brethren, Mennonites and the Society of Friends, committed themselves to a joint effort in exploring our common commitment to peacemaking. Working mostly on local and regional levels, the three groups have set goals of encouraging a renewed spiritual dedication to peacemaking, of clarifying and expressing our Biblical basis for peace, and of finding ways we can promote peacemaking in our society.

Many groups are working together in local areas. Is there a New Call group in your area? Does your church participate in this peacemaking effort? Ask your pastor or district peace counselor about their efforts.

Exchange programs In 1957, a group of Polish agricultural scientists arrived in the United States to study and do research. This was the beginning of a two-way exchange program which has since brought well over 500 such persons to study in our country and over 100 Brethren volunteers to go to Poland. Can you see what this has to do with international peacemaking?

Our exchange program helps achieve goals of building bridges of understanding, friendship and goodwill—

all making the prospects for world peace possible. Do you believe an exchange program is peacemaking? Do you know of youth exchanges? Would it be harder for you to go to war against some country if you had a close friend there?

Disasters and refugee work Disasters of all kinds occur around the world. Some are natural, like droughts, famines, earthquakes and floods. Some are caused by humans, like wars and political problems that cause people to leave their own countries and become refugees, searching for a homeland somewhere else in the world.

Our church has been active in placing refugees in local communities and in sending aid to war torn countries. Do you think this is a way to do peacemaking? Why or why not? Do we always have to say we are acting for peace? Can our actions alone promote trust and friendship?

Working with other churches Because our church is a member of both the National Council of Churches and the World Council of Churches, we have unusual opportunities to have a strong witness for peace included in their programs and policy statements. Members of our church have taken leadership in committees, both national and international, in planning programs, in delicate fact-finding tours to troubled areas, in writing papers, speaking and continually calling the attention of our government to questions of peace and disarmament.

Volunteers in troubled areas The Church of the Brethren has worked cooperatively with others in establishing reconciliation programs in troubled areas of the world. These programs are usually staffed by volunteers who have come through our BVS (Brethren Volunteer Service) training programs and are sponsored by the agencies to which they are assigned. These persons are located in places like Lebanon, the West Bank, Egypt, Ireland, Greece, Latin America, and other areas where there is conflict. They have an important responsibility. If there is a returned volunteer in your church or a neighboring church, you might want to talk with him or her about the work they did and how it contributed to peacemaking in the world.

WHAT YOU CAN DO

It isn't easy for *one* person, especially a youth, in the United States to think about international peacemaking. That's something we leave to our government and maybe our church leaders. Or is it? Let's take a look at some possibilities and maybe you can think of others.

Attitudes toward other peoples   What kind of person comes to your mind when someone mentions "Poles" or "Chicanos" or the Russians? We tend to form opinions about who people are, based on prejudice and misunderstanding.

We can work at better understanding by reading about people of other countries, about their music and art, their family life, schools, work, and churches. We can get to know those persons in our own community who are "different," include them in our activities and respect our differences.

Are there Vietnamese people in your community? Chicano farmworkers? Puerto Ricans? Are you getting to know them, appreciating who they are, eating their food and sharing your own?

Look at our life style   Our style of living is also important in international peacemaking. Ask yourself: How does my life style affect people in other places in the world? Would I be willing to give up my favorite food— chocolate, for instance—so that someone else could have a healthier life? Have you heard the saying, "Live simply so that others can simply live"?

Keeping up with current events   The news on TV is not the most pleasant hour of the day, but it does help you understand what's happening in our world. Most of our news media is geared to reporting from a United States viewpoint, so it is good to listen with a questioning attitude. We need to listen and read carefully and talk with others about what's happening. A good time to have such talks is in youth or church school class where you make some comparisons with the teachings of the Bible.

How about demonstrating? Some people feel this is one way to let others know when they don't approve of what's happening. It may or may not change anything, but it certainly calls attention to the issue. Just before the United States Congress was to vote on draft registration, many people carried signs in a steady walk in front of the White House. Others have had silent vigils before munitions plants. Some have protested arms sales to other countries by carrying signs at the Pentagon. Each person has to make his/her decision about such participation. Do you think it is a useful way to present your opinion?

Conclusion When others talk about national security, what is your response? We Christians have learned to put our trust and faith in God and in Jesus' way of love and peace. Is this faith applicable at all times or is it just for sermons and church discussions?

I believe the Bible teaches us to be peacemakers, to seek alternative ways of resolving conflict. We are called to be leaven or yeast. It only takes a little amount of yeast to make a whole pan of dough rise to overflowing. It helps me to remember that when I feel small or alone in my actions or beliefs.

We are all needed. We are all called. Peacemaking is urgently needed in today's world. Are you willing to accept some responsibility for the future of humankind?

ACTIVITIES

► Invite a former BVSer to talk about his/her work and how it related to peacemaking.
► Collect news stories and analyze them from the viewpoint of prophet Amos or Jesus.
► Study the 1980 Annual Conference resolution "A Time So Urgent."

- ► Let a few members of your group eat some delicious refreshments while all the others watch but have nothing. Talk about how that feels to all of you.
- ► Discuss security and what makes you feel really secure.
- ► Answer the questions asked about human rights, about the arms race, about demonstrations.
- ► List some actions you are willing to take to promote peace in the world.

CHAPTER 6

Registration
Charles L. Boyer

I don't want to march in the infantry,
Ride in the calvary,
Shoot the artillery,
If you want a war just don't call me
'Cause I've joined the Lord's army.

This version of an old World War I anti-war song reminds us that persons who have Christ as their King don't need to fight wars. Young adults under Christ's banner owe first allegiance to him. Allegiance to government comes after obedience to Christ.

But governments tend to forget that their laws are not as important as God's laws. Governments want Christians to believe that Jesus wasn't serious when he taught:
Turn the other cheek . . .

Go the second mile . . .

Love your enemies . . .

Put your sword back into its proper place. All those who take the sword die by the sword.

And because governments don't accept Christ's teachings they ask Christians to participate in killing.

Maximilian, a 21 year old young man, was drafted into the Roman army in 295 A.D. He refused to serve and explained his stand as follows: "I cannot serve as a soldier; I cannot do evil. I am a Christian." Sentence was pronounced, "Because you have, with a rebellious spirit, refused to bear arms you shall die by the sword." Maximilian was beheaded.

During the rise of Nazism in Europe a young Austrian farmer, Franz Jagerstatter, was drafted into Hitler's army. He refused to serve. On the day he was called to active duty he said goodbye to his family, served at mass at his village church and then walked alone to the next village to turn himself in at the police station. Jagerstatter was also beheaded for his strong stand against war.

Christians in the United States who are opposed to war don't face such severe penalties as befell Maximilian and Franz Jagerstatter. Our government recognizes that some persons because of strong religious and personal beliefs are conscientiously opposed to military involvement. If such persons are drafted they may request that right to perform an alternative service instead of joining the armed forces.

EVERY WHICH WAY BUT FIGHT

What choices are available today to a young person who is facing the military draft? The Church of the Brethren was founded by persons who believed that all war is sin. Because of that belief, members of the Church of the Brethren are encouraged not to volunteer for military duty. If drafted, Brethren face several options. Let me first mention three choices which our church does *not* encourage its members to use.

- Regular military participation for two or more years—this is what the government hopes draftees will accept when ordered to report for military duty. But since the Church of the Brethren teaches that all war is sin we cannot support the military involvement of our members.
- Performance of noncombatant duty for two years —the government provides one form of alternative

service called noncombatant work. Persons who accept this type of assignment enter the armed forces but refuse to carry or use weapons. They may serve as medics, office workers, cooks, and in other noncombat assignments. The Church of the Brethren feels that noncombatants within the armed forces are expected to do everything they can to build an efficient killing force. The church views that as contrary to God's will and encourages its members to avoid the noncombatant position.

- Acceptance of special deferments provided for ministerial students—our government has been willing to not draft young ministers and persons studying in seminaries. The Church of the Brethren believes that our ministers should accept no special privileges and should face conscription like all other members of the church. We believe in the priesthood of all believers and do not view ministers as more holy or God-fearing than anyone else.

POSSIBILITIES FOR PUZZLED PEACEMAKERS

Let me now share the two responses our denomination hopes its drafted members will choose:

- Request the conscientious objector classification and be prepared to serve alternative service in Brethren Volunteer Service or some other civilian not-for-profit service program.
- Openly and nonviolently choose not to cooperate with the drafting process and face the legal penalties for such action.

Since these are the responses our church believes are in keeping with Christ's teaching let us examine them in more detail.

First of all, if one chooses to become a conscientious objector what is involved? Is it difficult to convince a draft board that you are sincere? Will people call you a coward, a communist, or accuse you of being un-American?

If your religious faith, your understanding of the Bible, and your personal experiences of the presence of God lead you to oppose war you will likely not be in the majority position among your friends and classmates. If you speak out about your views and openly choose to become a conscientious objector, you can expect to be called a lot of uncomplimentary names. You will need to be firm in your beliefs and forgiving to those who try to put you down.

During a time of draft registration the conscientious objector can make an initial statement of opposition to war at age 18. At the time you sign a Selective Service registration form you should write, under your name, "I am a Christian conscientious objector to war." That will notify persons who read your card that you, already at age 18, are opposed to bearing arms. Try to obtain a photocopy of the registration card for your personal file. If the post office where you register does not have a copy machine, you should take the card elsewhere and return it after the copy has been obtained.

If you are drafted you will then need to defend your beliefs before a draft board. At the time you receive a draft notice to report for induction you are informed that a conscientious objector has a few days to appeal an induction order. It is very, very important that you promptly notify the proper officials that you are a conscientious objector and will not accept induction into the armed forces. Once you make this appeal you are entitled to a hearing with a draft board in your area.

CAN YOU PROVE IT?

Most draft boards are tough on conscientious objectors. They want to be sure that people believe what they say they believe. Some draft boards think most conscientious objectors are cowards. What kinds of questions do they ask? Here are some samples: What are the beliefs which are the basis for your claim as a conscientious objector? Would you be willing to enter the armed

forces and do noncombatant work? If not, why not?
Where did you learn these beliefs? Do your lifestyle and
actions show that you believe what you claim to believe?
If Christ didn't want Christians to fight why did he say
there will be wars and rumors of wars? What would you
do if someone attacked your mother or little brother?
Would you just look on or do nothing? What would happen if everyone believed like you? Wouldn't our enemies
overrun us? Here is a Bible. Can you show me where it
says Christians shouldn't fight for their country?

Could you answer those kinds of questions? It is obvious that persons opposed to participating in war need
to prepare ahead of time for this kind of grilling. How
can you get ready to defend your convictions so people
will see you know what you believe and you are not talking nonsense? Here are some very specific ways you can
work to strengthen your beliefs.

HOW TO GET HELP

First of all, obtain a form which lists the kinds of
questions draft boards ask. Most Church of the Brethren
pastors and youth leaders can give you such a form. If
nobody in your local church seems to have such material

you can obtain it by writing to our national offices. The address is: Peace Consultant, Church of the Brethren General Offices, 1451 Dundee Avenue, Elgin, IL 60120.

Once you receive this list of questions you will see that the form allows space for you to fill in your answers right on the same page. The questions, as we said earlier, are tough to answer. You may want to discuss your answers with your friends, parents, pastor, or youth counselors. When you have prepared your responses you can fill out the form making two copies. You should keep one copy and file the second copy with your local church or send it to the Brethren national offices using the address given in the previous paragraph.

Why go to all this trouble when you don't even know if you will ever be drafted? If you are drafted it will be up to you to prove you are a sincere conscientious objector to war. The fact that you took time to write out your beliefs will point to your sincerity. Also, the fact that you did it early, long before you were drafted, helps show you did not become a conscientious objector only because you saw your induction form in the mailbox.

Even if you never face a draft it is a good idea to file a conscientious objector form. When you accepted Christ and became a member of the Christian Movement you joined a peace movement. For over two hundred fifty years following Christ's death the Christian church taught pacifism and had a strong peace witness. Eventually the Christians gave up this peacemaking commitment and engaged in all kinds of wars where Christians killed Moslems, Jews, and other Christians. In 1708 our church was born, partly to provide a witness to Christian peacemaking. We believe the earliest Christians were right to accept pacifism as a way of life. We believe you and I should try to live as peacemakers wherever we find ourselves. In filling out a conscientious objector statement you are committing yourself to be a peacemaker wherever you are, whether or not you face a draft.

GETTING LETTERS OF REFERENCE

Once you have submitted a conscientious objector statement it is helpful if you can obtain three to five letters of reference. These should be one-page statements from people who know you well and who can confirm that you believe and act in peaceful ways. It is best if such persons are not relatives. Pastors, teachers, members of your church, and employers are good sources for such references. If you know someone who was in the military but respects your position, ask him or her to write a statement for you. That will certainly add support to your claim.

In the letters of references ask persons to indicate how long they have known you and in what relationship (i.e. your teacher, pastor, etc.). Next, they should tell why they believe you are sincere when you claim you would not participate in war. Finally, the writer may offer to appear as a witness for you if that would be helpful at some further time. These letters of reference should be filed along with your conscientious objector statement and you should make personal copies for your own record.

If you follow the above procedures to prepare yourself, you will very likely obtain a conscientious objector classification if you are drafted. Upon being granted this classification you will then be ordered to do alternative service work for two years.

Occasionally draft boards refuse to grant persons the right to perform alternative service after the conscientious objector claim is made and defended. If a draft board denies a claim for conscientious objector status, you can appeal to another regional board. Almost all sincere Christian conscientious objectors who appeal, and do not give up after one defeat, receive the desired classification from the second board.

Those ordered to perform alternative service work will be expected to work at least 40 hours per week and will be paid small wages. The government maintains lists of approved work projects. Brethren Volunteer Service has been one of those approved agencies.

CHOOSING NOT TO COOPERATE

Earlier I indicated that the Church of the Brethren also supports persons who openly and nonviolently choose to not cooperate with the registration and drafting processes. Why would Christians choose to go this route when the alternative service option is available? Isn't it dangerous to break the law and not register or report for alternative service? Are noncooperators lazy or selfish people who don't want to be bothered by others? Why sit in prison when you could be helping other people?

Until now there have not been large numbers of noncooperators in our church. This stance can be punishable by imprisonment and thousands of dollars in fines. Most Christians, even those who are opposed to military involvement, don't think noncooperation is the best alternative.

But there are increasing numbers of young adults who feel a bold, courageous witness must be made for peace. So long as conscientious objectors are a small number of people who remain quiet and don't protest their alternative service assignments the military efforts grind on. Noncooperators feel people must say "no" to the entire drafting system.

Bob Gross, a Brethren noncooperator during the Vietnam War, was imprisoned at Ashland, Kentucky. While in prison he wrote a poem to explain how he felt.

> I guess on the Persecution Continuum,
> I see myself somewhere in the middle

With the warmakers   And the dead children
on one end,   on the other.

Noncooperators may protest at various points. They may refuse to even register. Others protest by refusing to accept alternative service if it is offered. Some persons attempt to slow down the drafting process by encouraging others to not cooperate and by demonstrating against the draft. Noncooperators believe that if Jesus were here today he would not register with a system designed to prepare people to fight wars. Some will not pay taxes to buy weapons or train military personnel.

If you are a young woman or a young man not yet 18 years of age you need to think about registering with the government when you celebrate that magic eighteenth birthday. Only fellows have been expected to register for the draft in the past. Young women may also face registration in the future. And as you think of registering you must think of being drafted. How will you respond if called upon to train to kill other humans for whom Christ died? You need to ask yourself these questions:

- ▶ Can you picture Jesus armed with a rifle and bayonet?
- ▶ Can you agree to obey all orders given by a military chain of command and still obey Christ's commandment to love your enemies?
- ▶ Do you hate someone you have never seen so much that you are ready to kill her because you are told she is an ememy?

THREE QUESTIONS FOR PEACEMAKERS

Below are the questions you fill out if you are filing a conscientious objector preregistration form provided through our general offices. You may wish to formulate your answers and discuss these questions along with the above questions that conclude this chapter. The information provided in this handbook along with the Statement of the Church of the Brethren on War will help you in this process. Again, the actual form for your filing and the Statement on War may be obtained through the Church of the Brethren General Offices.

Question 1: *Describe the beliefs which are the basis for your claim for classification as a conscientious objector, and whether those beliefs would permit you to serve in a noncombatant position in the armed forces.*

This question asks you to describe, in detail and as forthrightly as possible, the basic principles by which you insist on guiding your life. You should describe those values which are of utmost importance to you as God, love, truth, etc., and why these beliefs are in conflict with military service. This question asks you to formulate your own statement of conscientious opposition to war. You should begin by saying that you are conscientiously opposed to war, and then describe why.

Question 2: *Describe how you acquired these beliefs.*

In answering this question, you should include any formal religious training you have had if you feel such training has helped you to arrive at your position. If you feel you believe as you do with no help from your formal training, there is no need to mention it. The influences of clergy, teachers, family members, books, membership in organizations are esential to list. Be specific; you must show that strong influences in your life have stimulated you to think seriously and clearly about participation in war.

Specific incidents can be included, such as demonstrations, seminars, or assemblies you have attended, to show that you believe as you do. Be careful not to give the impression that your beliefs are mainly "political."

Question 3: *Describe how your beliefs affect the way you live, and the type of work you do or plan to do.*

This is sometimes a difficult question for the young objector since he or she has not had experiences which can show deeply-held beliefs. Such a person should discuss how his or her future plans are deeply affected by a commitment to those beliefs. Describe kinds of employment you have had or plan to have which reflect your commitment. Discuss any public expressions, written or oral, you have given to your beliefs.

Describe your lifestyle, mention your life's goals as you have set them, and show how they are an outgrowth of your beliefs.

CHAPTER 7

A Peace Lab
David S. Young

In high school there are always smelly biology and chemistry labs. In them, students dissect animals or mix chemicals to see how the natural world operates. For those who continue in these fields of study, the laboratory becomes a more intense experience. Here future doctors work on animals before they operate on humans. Chemists first learn how to mix ingredients before they mix our prescriptions for the flu. The laboratory then becomes the training ground for the more practical day-to-day living.

Is there such a laboratory in which to learn the way of peace? Shouldn't there be somewhere youth could learn the methods and practice the techniques of peace-making? I believe that in our Brethren tradition the home and the church are the training grounds for peace-makers. The home is where we know others intimately, what we like about them and what we don't. We can either hurt each other or get along. The church is also a part of this laboratory where we learn the teachings of Jesus. Here we also work to get along with one another. In both settings we learn how to be peacemakers for the larger world.

I remember where I was taught the peace position of the church. I heard the teachings of Jesus in sermons, in Sunday school lessons, at home, and at church camp. But I also realize that the teachings were caught as well as taught. It was the quiet but sternly pleasant way my grandmother disciplined us boys that made an impression on me. There was the church where people worked together in choir, youth groups, church picnic, and the Love Feast. The impression made on me as a child was that we work together as Christians.

How can we learn a way of life that builds our ideals for peace? What rules need to be in the homes that teach peace? How could our church handle differences in a way that would convey the teachings of peace? How can we conduct ourselves so that our lives will be a positive witness, a constructive example, for the world in which we live? In this chapter we will answer these questions by looking at the way the Man of Galilee built peace. His spirit, his example are unique. We will look at three procedures in this chapter that would be in a laboratory of peace. Our hope is to become an agent for peacemaking in our world.

First Procedure: Upholding the Worth of Individuals

The first procedure for the church and the home, if they are to be the laboratory of peace, must be the upholding of the worth of each individual. We see this in the way Jesus handled the woman who was caught in adultery. There were people ready to kill her according to Jewish custom. Jesus said, "Let the one who is without sin among you be the first to throw a stone at her." After they all left, Jesus told the woman, "Neither do I condemn you; go, and do not sin again." Jesus upheld this woman when others would attack her. He also called her to live her life differently. When we hold up the value of each person in the home and in the church, we become a laboratory for making peace, and we ourselves become whole individuals.

A recent rerun of The Odd Couple showed this point well. In The Odd Couple, two bachelors, Oscar and Felix, share an apartment but have totally different interests. Felix decided that he was going to do a beautiful job as interior decorator of their apartment. He wanted to express his individuality and so made a concentrated effort to purchase a roomful of furniture that expressed his individuality.

He purchased two very modern chairs that looked like hands. A person could sit in the palm with the fingers serving as a back rest. The lounge chair was an uncomfortable-looking large curved surface resembling a potato chip lying down. A clock that showed different lights, instead of a face with hands, told the time. All to his satisfaction, the furniture was carefully put in place. Then Oscar came home.

We can only imagine the feelings that go with his disgust. There was nowhere to sit down except the potato chip-shaped chair that dumped him out promptly onto the floor. There was no suitable desk on which to write his sports news. So when Felix was gone, Oscar removed all the modern furniture and replaced it with old second-hand furniture. He bought an old couch, a lounge chair, and desk all in twenty minutes. He placed them in the living room. When Felix returned, he was furious and frustrated. His carefully planned design had been torn to pieces. This was the last straw. He could take other things like burnt toast and dirty floors but not ruining his creativity. He was ready to move out.

The resolution came, however, as Felix and Oscar decided to go out and buy their furniture together. Their whole gang of friends, who had seen the conflict brewing, then came to help them move the new furniture into their apartment. All were happy and delighted. They could get along after all. By recognizing each other's worth, a solution came into view.

Other People Matter   When we are set on our own way

or when we become upset, we often forget the worth of other people. We fly off the handle and let mom or dad have it. "You are the worst parents anybody could have." Sometimes we just disregard people in normal day-to-day living. We want to borrow our sister's jeans but we feel she will say no. So we just go to her room and get them. But then we are saying in effect, "You don't matter."

The kids at school are riding someone hard, perhaps even a teacher. At that point we have to decide if we will join in or buy out. I will never forget how a teacher in our high school was literally worn down by the class. The constant remarks, the water guns shot at him, the tricks — all got to him and he had a breakdown.

Working on people with continual destructive comments can have about the same effect as killing them. Paul's view of others still holds. "Do nothing from selfishness or conceit, but in humility count others better than yourselves (Philippians 2:3). The challenge is to uphold other people even when they have different ideas or when they do things with which we disagree. The first ground rule for the laboratory of peace is holding up the worth of each individual.

SECOND PROCEDURE: MAKING CONFLICT CONSTRUCTIVE

A second procedure in our laboratory is to handle conflicts constructively. Conflict and differences can be handled constructively or destructively. One common concern of youth today is that parents often do not get along at home. There is constant bickering and fighting. You may wonder, "How can I help mom and dad get along?" Further disillusionment comes to young people when they are getting ready for marriage. They say they never have learned a model for handling differences at home. Some young people then wonder if two people can ever get along. What does our Christian faith say about that?

The Scriptures do give direct teachings on solving differences. Conflict is part of living. How it is handled can be for growth or destruction of relationships. Someone in a conflict has to decide that he will stop arguing and begin to listen. This will take a special kind of individual who can think above the heat of the argument. Someone has to swallow his pride and decide not to have the last word. Issues need not be swept under the rug, but problems must be clearly delineated. To decide to disagree is very important. In fact, this is the second ground rule. Discussion must occur.

Ring Trouble   Handling differences constructively and discussing issues becomes even more important as we choose that person we will marry. I was recently sitting with a couple not yet married who were getting into conflict over choosing their wedding ring. He wanted white gold and she, yellow gold. I reviewed with them the steps that go into making a decision. One had gone ahead to the store and picked out his choice. I said that we need to get in on the ground floor of an issue together. On any large decision we need to go together to decide. Then we need to discuss and look at the item from all sides, hearing the other partner's likes and dislikes. If we can't respect and listen to someone else and then discuss our viewpoints, we will run into trouble later.

A mutually agreed-upon solution must be found. As a decision is made, we should both be settled on it. Never again, not in one year or in ten years, is it fair to say that we didn't get what we wanted. Thus we avoid accumulated feelings of anger that later fester and explode. We work at peace in our homes. In establishing our own home, we make a second ground rule that we will discuss together items that arise. First ground rule . . . to uphold the other person always. Second ground rule . . . discuss each item to come to some agreement.

Results vs. Insights   Jesus himself calls for working out one's differences. In the sermon on the Mount Jesus says, "You have heard that it was said to those of old, 'You shall not kill; and whoever kills shall be liable to judgment.' But I say to you that everyone who is angry with his brother shall be liable to judgment; whoever insults his brother shall be liable to the council, and whoever says 'You fool!' shall be liable to the hell of fire" (Matthew 5:21, 22). What Jesus is concerned about is the deep-seated anger that leads to spiteful and demeaning comments. Issues must be dealt with before relationships degenerate to this point. Discussion and compromise in the best sense of the word must occur.

The same needs to happen in the church. One of the outstanding impressions made on me as a youth was the way in which our family handled disagreements in the church. We attended the Sunday school where teachers fostered discussion of different ideas on all kinds of topics. The old pews were moved, and not very easily, from a lecture-type setting to a circle for face-to-face encounter. I can well remember attending as a youth an elective class where I heard the adults of my church talk about how they worked at differences in marriage. A great impression was made on me that these people worked on getting along. It instilled in me a Christian spirit needed to work at differences. I also learned that Christians can actually enjoy each other. It was okay to have different points of view; it was also a lot of fun to learn how to get along. And there was good humor.

Pew Power   In the same regard, never in my home did I hear a degrading comment about church members. We talked about what needed doing or joined in to help the church. I was taught that one reason to go to church was to grow to be like Jesus. Each of us was to take personal responsibility for ourselves and for the church to grow in this fashion. We knew that there were differences, but people were not run down in the process.

This led me to try to help my youth counselors. They were ready to throw in the towel at several points. I can remember trying as a youth to give them encouragement or show them appreciation. Now I realize that my efforts were a part of the very peace stance of the church. Anger was never directed against individuals. I find the church an exciting place in which to work because of this background that solved problems but didn't kill people by words in the process. Constructive handling of differences is this second essential procedure.

THIRD PROCEDURE: WHAT ABOUT LOVE?

And finally, there is a third ground rule that operates in this laboratory. This is a chemistry that is unique. This is the chemistry of love. Perhaps what is really unique in this laboratory is a spirit, a climate. It is more than steps and procedures. The lab is known for its smell. The way of peace is a style, an attitude, a process. Because our personalities are different, we will go about this differently. But we are called to a climate that teaches peace in its very manner.

In talking to couples before marriage, I try to help them find their pattern for disagreeing and for making up. It helps to learn how we operate under stress. It also helps us learn how to be reconciled. Some of us seem like turtles. When we get angry we go into our shell, and then someone must use a crowbar to get us out. Others of us are like a skunk; we shoot others. I imagine skunks are very lonely animals. Who in your relationship begins the process of making up? As a turtle person, how can I stretch out more? As a skunk, how can I hold my fire when things get rough? In short, how can we build a climate that will make for peace?

Imitation Killing This chemistry of love will infiltrate into every aspect of our home life. As a child we were taught that even the games we played had an influence on us. We were forbidden to play with toy guns because of the climate it created. Even imitation killing teaches a way that is unhealthy. I was not totally happy with that

rule. In fact, on one occasion my brother and I secretly got money from our allowance and went to the store and purchased two cap guns.

It was about bedtime when my mother knew something was wrong. Shamefully we brought out our toy guns. We were not spanked. We had to do the harder thing. Return the guns. The next day came, and we timidly took our guns back to the store. The clerk asked many questions, of course. Finally, to our relief, she gave our money back. I was taught more by this example than I realized. By our actions we would not imitate the way of war.

I was also saved from danger by this rule. I later learned that one day when the neighborhood boys were playing, an accident occurred. Near our home was a large well that had a building around it to prevent anyone from falling in the water. One day, when the fellows were playing guns, one boy came around the corner of the well house. He shot. Only this time it was a B-B gun that he had in his hand, and the pellet hit the eye of his friend. My classmate received a glass eye to replace the good eye lost in the innocent game.

CONCLUSION: FINDING OUR WAY OF PEACE-LIVING

We are challenged to develop a character and personality that makes for peace. There are always certain persons in a group who bully others and so create a hardship. There are also persons who cause dissention because of their personal needs. But the youth who really stands up for what he or she believes and also treats others fairly can make all the difference in any group.

In our youth group in Southern district of Pennsylvania there was one high school student who always seemed to draw a crowd around him. I asked another youth in the group what made this one boy so popular. The reply was that this young person didn't compromise himself by doing wrong; he didn't misuse others, and he had a likable sense of humor. He had it all together we would say today. And because of that he set the pace for friendships.

In the book of James, we see why we fight. "Where do all the fights and quarrels among you come from? They come from your desires for pleasure, which are constantly fighting within you. You want things; but you cannot have them, so you are ready to kill; you strongly desire things, but you cannot get them, so you quarrel and fight" (James 4:1, 2 Good News). James sees how the desires for things and the emotions of greed and envy lead to fighting. It's not the clothes other kids have or the car they own that really makes the difference. It's who we are that is the most important. Keeping our values at the right place will lead us to the happiest life.

Shaped by Love The Scriptures call for wholehearted obedience to Christ, and then our human relationships will clear up. We will put less emphasis on what we want and more emphasis on seeking what God wants and what we can do together. Ultimately this is what we are called to do. We are invited by Christ to make life in him our single aim. We want to have our personalities shaped around his gentle but firm spirit of love.

In this chapter we have explored three ground rules that go into the making of peace. We have called the home and the church the laboratory where these rules should be lived and learned. Rule one is to hold up the worth of each individual. Rule two is to discuss differences in order to work out a solution. Rule three is to apply a unique spirit, a chemistry of love as we're calling it, to each situation. Thus we will be building a constructive environment in whatever situation we are in. In all of this we will learn of Christ.

This is where our statement of war begins anyway. "The Church of the Brethren seeks by processes of education and spiritual nurture to help its members to allow a spirit of peace and an attitude of nonviolence to develop within themselves as an outgrowth of deep religious conviction. They are encouraged to demonstrate this spirit in their daily relationships in the home, the school, business, and the community. We seek thereby to lead individuals into such intimate contact with Jesus Christ, our Lord, that they will commit themselves to him and to the manner of life which he taught and exemplified." In learning the way of peace we ourselves grow to be more like Christ. We, the products, will be agents of his peace in the world.

FOR DISCUSSION

▶ Do you agree that the church and the home should be like a laboratory for learning the way of peace?

▶ Discuss the three gbround rules suggested for this laboratory. What others would you add? Where have you seen these rules work/fail?

▶ If you are in a room mark off two areas. Ask each youth to decide if he or she is a skunk or a turtle. Have the individuals choose their point in the continuum. Discuss.

CHAPTER 8

Vision for Peace
M. R. Zigler

War is like a game between two athletic teams organized and supported by two groups of people. There must be a winner so therefore there must be a loser. The team getting the most goals is clearly the winner.

Each player accepts the struggle for his team against the other.

Each team spends many hours practicing.

Excitement increases.

The two community bands prepare for the occasion and are located at different positions on the athletic field. Likewise, the twirlers representing the two teams come to the game to sing, dance, and lead the people of the two communities to praise their players and boo the opposing team. When the game is finished the losing team approaches the winners and shakes hands and probably says, "We will win next year." Many times the two teams are given a banquet together to finish the experience and to honor each player for a fine performance. Athletic teams represent young men and young women, supported enthusiastically by their parents and neighbors.

WAR IS A DIFFERENT GAME

The winning team is the one that actually kills the most people or injures their bodies and minds so that they cannot continue as soldiers. The participants are citizens called to serve the nation. They must go through terrific training and must be committed to kill the persons representing the enemy. A soldier is committed to obey the command of officers to go into the territory of the enemy knowing that he may never return, and if not killed, may be taken as a prisoner of war. The bands and the twirlers serve in the celebrations when persons are being trained, as they go forward toward the battlefield, and when they come marching home after the war is finished. The citizens who die in battle are honored. They do not attend the banquet at the end of the war game. The losing team is crushed and suffers severe penalties. The winning army and the supporters must rebuild what has been destroyed. Everyone loses.

LIFE IS SACRED

Perhaps the most sacred event in the total life of a human being is the creating of a child. One superior experience a mother enjoys that a father cannot is to feel a living, growing boy or girl in her body for nine months. Neither can the father feel the thrill of the actual birth, delivering a child to the world like a mother. The coming of a child is always good news for the family, the community, the nation and the church.

When a child is born, the family registers the event and the state accepts the name of the baby presented by the parents. The government or the state assumes the responsibility to care for the child in many ways. Laws are developed as guidelines for the creating of loyal citizens. Perhaps the most outstanding gifts of the nation are education and protection. Regardless of the life profession chosen, be it farmer, merchant, doctor, mortician, lawyer, teacher, taxi or truck driver, guidelines are developed and made available for every individual to provide a peaceful way to live together in the communities of the nation. A change happens, however, when war is declared. Then the state demands the life unreservedly, and all resources necessary for a war are ordered to be surrendered.

When people find they must live together to survive they inevitably need to find an explanation for existence. Therefore, the idea comes naturally that there had to be a "creator" for all things. Then they worship and together they feel that every person has a divine origin equal with all other persons they meet. Through this comes a vision for the common good. They set goals for united achievement feeling that all creation is a divine order. Only those who feel this common experience enjoy a common vision. Only those who choose to join the search for the future can be counted in this body that is different from the state. We call this "the Church."

This community of believers is really a community within the community called a state. Humanly speaking the unanswered question is, "Who owns the child?" The state? The Church? The father and mother are citizens and live under the guidance of the state. The Church offers membership on a voluntary agreement to follow Christ and his teachings. Both Church and state demand loyalty as long as they live, even to death. Therefore, each individual is a member of the state and can be a member of the Church. Great decisions have to be made to be a true citizen and a loyal church person.

JESUS AND THE DIFFERENT WAY

Jesus, the founder of the Church, had to find his life way at a time when war methods controlled his nation. He had to choose between what was right and what was wrong as he lived under the guidelines as a citizen and as a religious person. Therefore, it is very important to understand both the secular and the religious life of Jesus. Jesus was born a boy who "increased in wisdom and in stature, and in favor with God and Man." He developed a strong body and a creative mind. He felt at home with God, and people loved him. Because he loved, he set an example of a superior life. It was prophesied in the Old Testament that such a person would be called the Prince of Peace. During the excitement at his birth, his parents and neighbors heard the voices praising God and saying, "Glory to.God in the highest, and on earth peace, goodwill toward men." This event is honored on December 25th every year, when we sing Christmas carols around the world. We sing the Halleluia Chorus in our homes, our churches, and also at community festivals, and even in stores and on the street as we seek gifts for the members of our families and neighbors.

During the entire lifetime of Jesus the religious body he represented was under the control of a foreign power with military force. Jesus called twelve people to be his disciples by simply asking them, "Come, follow me." It was understood that each disciple gave up everything and listened to the teachings of Jesus about his kingdom on earth, which could not be understood by the citizens representing the government. This created conflict between the followers of Jesus and their neighbors so they inquired of him how they should answer the question of relationship between the government and Christ's teaching. Christ responded, "Render unto Caesar the things that are Caesar's and unto God the things that are God's." This is a very difficult question and the answer is also difficult. Both the government and the church expect complete allegiance. In wartime, nations call all citizens to participate. The answer that Jesus gave is not specifically referring to war, but it does describe a Christian as citizen and as a disciple.

Naturally in wartime, individuals decide whether or not they will serve in the military, which is designed to enter the war game to kill enemies, or to humbly request the opportunity to live and promote peace without violence. A difficult problem occurs because citizens loyal to the state at war cannot appreciate a person who refuses to enter the military. It is also difficult for the person who decides that he cannot participate fully to understand the soldier. The business of Christian people is to allow religious liberty and to promote reconciliation between these two points of view. The decision involved cannot be postponed or evaded.

Jesus was asked by his disciples, "What is the greatest commandment?" He replied, "Thou shall love your God with all thy heart, body, soul and mind and thy neighbor as thyself." The principle of love is the basic presentation of Christ and is way of life. Jesus said, "On this rock (referring to love) I will build my church."

CHURCH AND GOVERNMENT

Governments are designed to maintain peace through military force. The Christian Church is designed to implement "On Earth Peace" through love. When this message prevails, war is unthinkable. The ultimate goal of both Church and state must be to seek a world of creative citizenship whereby governments can live together without war. Government must seek the will of all citizens. The Church must teach its members to adjust to human problems by non-violent methods. Both are responsible for the creation of a society whereby a child can be born and live a life without fear.

Therefore, an alternative method must be discovered by the Christians to avoid sinning. It is a tragedy that it must be recorded that even until this time Christians agree to kill one another to settle tensions. It is difficult to imagine that Catholics will kill Catholics; Lutherans will kill Lutherans; likewise Presbyterians, Methodist. Most churches in the last decade have endured many discussions concerning the sacredness of life dealing with the subject of abortion. The hope is that someday the sacredness of life will control decisions in such a way that all problems will be settled by negotiation and arbitration.

I have never consulted a soldier who really wanted

war. Neither have I contacted any governmental official who desired war. People who argue for defense wish that the money spent could be used for useful advantages of all citizens. Yet there seems to be some force that exalts the game of war and seems to satisfy and, according to historical records, glorify killing. Actually, advocates for war believe that war is a justifiable peacemaking and peace keeping method. This position is difficult to be maintained among Christians but the Old Testament declares, "Thou shall not kill." And the New Testament "On Earth Peace."

A PERSONAL STORY

I was born November 9, 1891, just 27 years after the close of the Civil War which divided many denominations in the United States into what is called "North and South churches." Few denominations have corrected that division. My birth occurred in Virginia, and therefore I have a southern interpretation for that conflict among Christians. So many real personal stories were told me that I almost felt like I was alive during the Civil War. One very small evidence of this conflict was a half-burned log above the manger in a horse stable. On inquiry, my father stated that the army of the North had set fire to burn the stable. My grandfather was able to extinguish the fire before the building could be destroyed. This is a small illustration, but everytime I looked at that burned log as a youth, it gave me pain that a person could even think about doing such an act.

When the Spanish American War challenged men to go to war, I recall my mother weeping because my brother was considering accepting the call. I can remember the very large pictures of three Admirals that were given to me by recruiters, which I placed on the walls of my bedroom. I was born in a Church of the Brethren community. I knew by listening to conversations that if I desired to be a member in the Church of the Brethren I would have to make a decision that I would not go to

war as long as I lived. I heard the ministers of the Church asking the question at baptism, "Will you promise not to participate in war or learn the art of war?" The Church of the Brethren from its beginning in 1708 held the position against war without reservations. By the time of the first world war I had made this promise and was baptized.

Immediately when the United States entered the war, a conflict between Church and state became real. Action had to be taken by the leaders of the church to consult men of government. I was exempt because I was working with the United States Marines as a YMCA Secretary, a civilian organization, as a staff member for religious and recreational programs. This was a great experience living with ten thousand soldiers on Parris Island for three years. This was the "war to end all wars." Several commanding officers in conversation with me placed the blame of the war on the churches for not preventing the first world war. This experience gave me a firm commitment that the church must dedicate all resources, life and means, to peacemaking efforts.

HELPING THE CHURCH DO ITS JOB

When the war was ending and I was thinking about future work, I could not overcome the desire that the church just might eliminate war as a peacemaking method. Then the teaching of my childhood came back to me distinctly. The Church of the Brethren had made a desperate effort to imitate Christ and to be obedient to His teachings as revealed in the New Testament. I heard the ministers quote the scriptures, "Thou shall not kill. Love your enemies. When a person would ask you that you go with him one mile, go with him two. If he should ask for a coat, give him an overcoat also." Searching sermons were preached against being offended by anyone, and for seeking forgiveness for any offense. In fact, it was understood that a member should not accept communion as long as reconciliation could not be achieved. At baptism it was stressed that we should use the method described in Matthew 18 to settle human problems. If it was not possible to have peace between the parties concerned, the case should be referred to the church council for final action. Therefore, I have a firm conviction that this method should be used for settling national and international contests.

Because of the teaching of my church and my experience in the first world war, I decided to accept the call to serve my church as Home Mission Secretary. I felt that this would be one way I could do my part to eliminate war as a peacemaking method, but it was very clear that the Church of the Brethren was too small and needed help to proclaim peace on earth without war. Therefore, it seemed inevitable that the message of the Church of the Brethren for peace should be delivered to the world in obedience to the "Great Commission" and that everything possible should be done to unite Christians to move together to maintain peace.

WHAT IS A NISBCO?

The great objective announced during the first world war, "A war to end all wars," registed a failure when the second world war was declared by the President of the United States. He had promised that no one would be sent abroad to fight a foreign war. Leaders of the three Historic Peace Churches (Mennonites, Friends, Brethren) called a meeting in 1935 to consider peacemaking and to promote the idea of preventing wars. Therefore, this fellowship was prepared for the announcement of the second world war. Leaders of the nation requested that all bodies interested in the exemption from war for religious reasons should unite as one body to consult with government officials regarding alternatives to be a creative citizen as an expression of loyalty.

This experience involved the principle of church-state separation. At the same time the National Service Board for Religious Objectors was recognized as a bridge between the interests of the state and churches. Religious liberty, the greatest gift recognized in the Constitution of the United States, was actively granted to deal with the problems of the draft for military purposes. A National Service Board for Religious Objectors was organized by a representative from the Mennonites, Friends, Brethren, Federal Council of Churches for Christ in America, the Fellowship of Reconciliation and two persons to represent conscientious objectors in other denominations.

These seven representatives established a procedure known as Civilian Public Service which provided an alternative satisfactory to both Church and state. This established a pattern that lasted through smaller wars and is a basic experience to determine procedures in case of a renewal of the registration and draft that might be considered the beginning of a third world war. The National Service Board for Religious Objectors now operates under a changed name, recognizing the fact that there are 47 different organizations uniting to create one voice to approach the United States government for further consideration in our mutual relationships. The new name is National Interreligious Service Board for Conscientious Objectors. This cooperative experience has continued unbroken since 1940.

TAKING NEXT STEPS TOGETHER

Every year the President of the United States and the Congress review the defense strength for the nation, and they authorize a military and financial program for the defense of the nation. Also appropriations are made for peacemaking by the State Department. There seems to be a constant threat that arbitration to settle international disturbances will fail, and therefore it is argued that a larger commitment of persons and means must be authorized for national safety. It is reasonable, therefore, that the increasing number of pacifists and conscientious objectors must unite for strength to prevent war, to plan for the future, to earn the right to accept religious liberty, and to be considered as loyal citizens.

Since there is no organization that binds Christian denominations together, responsibility rests upon each church to speak officially. Therefore, the Church of the Brethren must become stronger and offer strength to create a voluntary unity to promote a movement against the threat of war. Under the Lordship of Christ, the Prince of Peace, we must be faithful to the Great Commission to teach peacemaking methods and to avoid violent hostility, actually killing persons, to determine the solution of a conflict. Annually a church must review its heritage, measure its achievements, and agree to next steps toward a world without war. For the good of everyone everywhere in the world the resources for destruction must be used for the good life.

Thereby, we will be following Christ according to his life description "He went about doing good." Let the nations beat their swords into plowshares and refuse to use violence. Every minute of time is one-half history and the

other half future. There is no escaping making decisions, for the future is always present and time waits for no one. Therefore the Church must always be obedient to the challenge "to go on to perfection." A church must have a vision for the future and faithfully act to achieve the goal of "a world at peace."

Summary

As disciples of Christ, we must unite our strength intellectually and spiritually in order to be obedient to the last command of Christ to go forth baptizing people everywhere and teaching his way of life. Therefore, it is a fact that we must move into the future practicing the presence of Christ as a church, simply "doing good."

It is imperative that we be obedient to the last command of Jesus, "The Great Commission:"

Now the eleven disciples went to Galilee, to the mountain to which Jesus had directed them. And when they saw him they worshiped him; but some doubted. And Jesus came and said to them, "All authority in heaven and on earth has been given to me. Go therefore and make disciples of all nations, baptizing them in the name of the Father and of the Son and of the Holy Spirit, teaching them to observe all that I have commanded you; and lo, I am with you always to the close of the age."

Matthew 28:16-20

When we accept this challenge we will fervently worship together with the Lord's Prayer at the center:

Our Father who art in heaven, hallowed be Thy name;
Thy Kingdom come, Thy will be done on earth as it is in heaven.
Give us this day our daily bread;
Forgive us our debts, as we forgive our debtors.
Lead us not into temptation, but deliver us from evil;
For thine is the kingdom and the power and the glory forever. Amen

If all these petitions are answered, there will be

peace on earth. These petitions must be more sincerely felt and answers must be expected.

We will then leave our worshiping together and live in communities as dedicated church persons and creative citizens avoiding conflict, remembering the benediction:

> Now may the grace of God, the fellowship of Christ and the gift of the Holy Spirit be with you.

We will unite our strength with all Christian bodies to eliminate armed conflict. It is essential to announce that all Christians seek the support of other faiths in eliminating both the preparation for war and war itself. To build a strong continuing church must require a baptismal vow that members will neither participate in war nor learn the art of war. A church for the future must have a strong dedicated youth, supported by the congregations, prepared to stand the test inevitably made at times of registration and conscription. War indicates defeat, and therefore the work of the church is definitely in peacetime, always working unitedly to prevent armed conflict. Preventing war means to give an active peace testimony, a practicing of the presence of Christ as a member of his church and as a loyal citizen of a nation that grants religious liberty.

QUESTIONS

- ▶ Explain how it is possible to be a faithful church member and a loyal citizen?
- ▶ Should the Church of the Brethren, a Peace Church, require for church membership a vow neither to participate in war nor learn the art of war?
- ▶ Should the Church of the Brethren have a voluntary service program for youth to give a peace testimony during peacetime?
- ▶ Who owns the child at birth?
- ▶ Discuss the statement in the chapter, "preventing war means to give active peace testimony." Make

a list of occupations that encourage world peace.
Make a list of steps your church could take to give
active peace testimony.

The Shalom Community
Robert W. Neff

You may be thinking, "Why did Bob begin a chapter on the 'Shalom Community' with a 'Peanuts' comic strip? It doesn't sound like peace and doesn't say very much about how we should get along. You may even wonder how Snoopy could have any peace with all that commotion. Each member of his body is quarreling with the other. The heart says, "It's a stout heart that counts." The leg says, "I am only a leg." There's even name calling, "It's that stupid fat stomach." "Not much peace and quiet if you ask me," you might be saying to yourself.

I don't know whether Charles Schulz had Paul's letter to Corinth in mind, but it surely sounds like Chapter 12 of First Corinthians to me. Paul talks in that chapter about a healthy Christian body, namely the community of believers. He uses the example of the human body to talk about the obstacles to our getting along as well as what develops a strong and peaceable Christian fellowship.

We discover in I Corinthians 12 and in the Snoopy cartoon that when each member is out for itself, there are problems. Paul states, "My body does not consist of one member but many." This statement means that we should learn how we relate to other parts of the body. A sound healthy body requires our living for each other. I can't say to myself "Me First!" Paul encourages us to remember that we are part of a group in which each of us has a significant role to play.

Let me give an illustration. We have a very dear friend, Martha, who used to live as we did in a housing co-operative known as the York Center Co-op. Martha had the great ability to listen to everyone and to take people seriously. Right before our family moved to Elgin in 1978, Martha came back to the Co-op for a visit as we were packing up our things in preparation for the movers. Martha told us that she wasn't too sure what her contribution in life was. She didn't feel like she exercised any great gifts. I said, "Martha we have missed you so much; everyone has! The Co-op has not been the same without you. You had a listening ear. We felt heard and understood. That's a great gift."

We may not think we are important but we are. God has given us each a gift to be used for one another and not just for ourselves. Martha is a listening person. That's why she means so much to all of us. She did not keep the gift for herself but used it for others. That's what makes a healthy body.

Sometimes we see a person who plays basketball or baseball well. We may be tempted to think, "Unless I am a good athlete, I am not worth anything." Paul says not all of us need be athletes or cheerleaders or bookworms. If all of us were the same thing, where would the body be? A school would not have a football team if everyone were a quarterback on that team. We need to recognize our differences and not yield easily to peer pressure which would cause us to be someone other than who we are. If you have a good ear, be a musician or a good listener. By all means use that gift for others. Don't be like the members on Snoopy's team.

Be careful not to say to a friend, "We can't get along because you're different." As Paul says, "One eye cannot say to the hand, I have no need of you. Or again, the head to the feet, I have no need of you." We do not need to be the same. It's hard to get along with people who are different than we are. Yet Paul tells us that's what life is all about.

Paul ends this chapter with the observation, "If one member suffers, all suffer together; if one member is honored, all rejoice together." That's a far cry from what each member of the body was saying while Snoopy was jogging. It's easy when someone is suffering to walk away and forget them. When someone wins an award, it's easy to say, "She didn't deserve it." Those actions don't make a healthy body.

In 1977 I attended a worship service at the Ebenezer Baptist Church in Atlanta, Georgia where the father of Martin Luther King was pastor. After a soprano sang a beautiful solo, we politely clapped. Martin Luther King, Sr. told us that we were very polite but lacked much enthusiasm for a soloist who had poured her heart out. "It would have taken my congregation a full five minutes to quiet down after a song like that." We may be reluctant to show support to someone who performs well. Paul says rejoicing with another person who is celebrating is what life together is all about.

When someone is hurting, we may be afraid to ask what's wrong. We may feel that we don't know what to say. Even worse, we may not want to become involved. A Christian peacemaker shows care and concern by simply sharing with a person when they are hurt. We know when others care by the way they stand with us in our time of trouble.

Peacemaking begins with the person next to us, our neighbor. We can act like the members of Snoopy's body, warring with one another and caring only for ourselves. Or we can see ourselves as members of a larger body, each with a role to play, each in need of one another, each supporting the other. We shall know Christ by the new community, the Shalom Community, in which we are all called to share. That community extends around the world with differences as large as the human heart, but none so great that they can't fit into the hand of God. Peacemaking with the person next door leads to peacemaking around the world. Peacemaking begins at home and leads to the throne of God.

SOMEBODY

Words & Music by Andy Murray
Arranged by Terry Murray

Bibliography

GENERAL:

Arnett, Ronald, *Dwell in Peace* Elgin: Brethren Press 1980

Church of the Brethren Annual Conference, *A Statement of the Church of the Brethren on War, Revised* Elgin: Brethren Press 1970

Lamoreau, John and Ralph Beebe, *Waging Peace: A Study in Biblical Pacifism* Newberg, Oregon: Barclay Press 1980

McSorley, Richard, *New Testament Basis of Peacemaking* Washington, D.C.: Center for Peace Studies 1979

Peachey, J. Lorne, *How to Teach Peace to Children* Scottdale, Pa.: Herald Press 1981

BIOGRAPHIES:

JOHN KLINE

Funk, Benjamin, *Life and Labors of Elder John Kline* Elgin: Brethren Press 1963

Sappington, Roger, *Courageous Prophet* Elgin: Brethren Press 1964

ALEXANDER MACK

Willoughby, William, *Counting the Cost* Elgin: Brethren Press 1979

TED STUDEBAKER

Royer, Howard, "Ted Studebaker, A Dissenter from Despair" *Messenger* Vol. 120 No. 12 pp 4-5

DAN WEST

Yoder, Glee, *Passing on the Gift* Elgin: Brethren Press 1978

JEAN ZIMMERMAN

Simmons, Steve, "Jean Zimmerman Lives a Vision" *Messenger* Vol. 128 No. 5 pp 12-15